T5-ACP-132

Musings of a Catholic Street Evangelist

This Book is on loan from the reading room at Our Lady of Refuge:
3750 Commerce Rd,
West Bloomfield, MI 48324

Enjoy this book for up to 3 weeks, and then kindly return it! For the enjoyment of others please <u>do not</u> highlight or write on the pages ☺

Musings of a Catholic Street Evangelist

Tools and Tips for Evangelization Success

Donna Phipps

Musings Of A Catholic Street Evangelist:
Tools And Tips For Evangelization Success
Copyright © 2016 by Donna Phipps

All rights reserved. No part of this book may be used or reproduced in any form, electronic or mechanical, including photocopying, recording, or scanning into any information storage and retrieval system, without written permission from the author except in the case of brief Quotation embodied in critical articles and reviews.

Printed in the United States of America

The Troy Book Makers • Troy, New York • thetroybookmakers.com

To order additional copies of this title, contact your favorite local bookstore or visit www.tbmbooks.com

ISBN: 978-1-61468-337-7

Acknowledgements

Thank you to my team mates with whom I share this adventure.

Thanks be to God for allowing us to be on this adventure!

Contents

Introduction 1
What is Evangelization? 3
Prayer 7
The Work of Evangelization 17
Building the Evangelization Team 27
Setting Goals and Objectives 39
Event Planning 47
Limiting Factors 65
Street Evangelization 85
Musings and Lessons Learned 101
Musings On People 111
Social Justice 117
Final Thoughts 133
Appendix A 137
Appendix B 149
Appendix C 155
Appendix D 161
Appendix E 167
Epilogue 169

Introduction

Here it is. Another book on Evangelization. Why do we need yet another book? I will begin by saying that as a fledgling in Catholic Evangelization, I read every book there was on Evangelization. I found them all to be somewhat lacking in specifics. They spoke of target audiences and church involvement and demographics, but not one mentioned any concrete ideas to get started with. I have read some of these other books and been left with the feeling of "ok so where do I begin?" and "how does this apply to me and my understanding of what I can do?" So I am writing this book for all who are out there struggling with these very questions, who want to build up our beautiful Catholic Church but just don't know how to begin. I have also included things I have learned along the way, my understanding, and even many of my mistakes to, hopefully, be a more concrete source of inspiration to you. God bless you in your endeavors. Keep your chins up, smiles on your faces and joy in your hearts.

1
What is Evangelization?

So what is Evangelization? The United States Conference of Catholic Bishops (USCCB) wrote a document called <u>Go and Make Disciples</u> several years ago on what Evangelization means. The summary of the information contained therein is threefold:

1. Build up the knowledge of the Faith and the confidence of the people who are already attending Mass regularly.

2. Speak to those outside of the sphere of the Church, either Protestant or no religious affiliation and draw them in to a knowledge and love of Jesus.

3. Let your fingers do the talking so that by your works with the poor, marginalized, and those down on their luck that they may be able to see the love of God shining through you.

Sounds easy enough right? In one sense, it's the easiest thing in the world to do. If you love God, Jesus, The Holy Spirit and His Church, it's easy to let it become a normal and natural extension of your very life and self. You bring God with you wherever you go, and it's not just reserved for church on Sundays. God is so much a part of you that you know He is with you in all situations, good and bad, each and every day.

Sorry to say though, most Catholics don't have that type of love for God or relationship with Him. God, oftentimes, is just relegated to Sundays or to the social sphere of church and doesn't extend to all aspects of life. It's not easy for us to reach and grow beyond our comfort zones. I believe God calls us to do just that. He knows what we can become and how we can be our very best selves. The key to that is trust in His guidance and a willingness to grow. I had lunch with a friend of mine who summarized, what I thought was quite well, what it means to be a disciple of Christ. He said "you need to be flexible, available, teachable, dependable and committed to Him." God likes to throw curve balls at us. They help us grow past ourselves and expand our thinking. In any situation that occurs in your life, you can ask "what is God trying to teach me here?" And then trust in God and see where he leads you. It is always an adventure when you trust in Him! Trust takes time and perseverance. Fortunately, we have a patient and generous Holy Spirit who has given us all the gifts we need to journey with God. We can always ask God for more of a particular gift where we feel lacking, and He will generously fill your request because He wants you to be close to Him.

If you are reading this book, you have stirrings in your heart that you want to do something more for God, to build His Church etc. I hope this book

What Is Evangelization?

will be a useful tool for you as you stumble along the road of faith and the adventure of Evangelization. It's not a straight and clear-cut line. There are a lot of zig zags and pitfalls along the way with disappointments. But disappointments can also be lessons learned for future endeavors. And failures can be opportunities to go in a different direction.

In these pages I will list and talk about some of the tools and tips that will help you on your way to making a great Evangelization team, building up the faith in your individual church and exploring new and creative ways to get the Word out. Each parish has a personality and a vision of its own, and no one program fits all. But God's love does. God's love is embracing and knows no bounds and is available to everyone who seek Him. His Church also is a haven for all of us who are lost and in need of Him and His Sacramental and healing presence. People are always seeking God, even though they don't realize it. They fill their time with extremes trying to fill the empty spots in their hearts. Yet it is God who is the only thing that can fill people's hearts. It is up to us to let people know there is hope and consolation waiting for them, if they just reach out for it.

This is not a book written for intellectuals or those who want to be filled with facts and statistics. It is a book written by a simple soul, looking to connect with others at a very basic and simple level to help spread the Word of God in this hurting world. You can get statistics from other sources. Most of this book is based on personal experience and conversations with friends who are out there doing the work of Evangelization.

In the following chapters, I will explore the importance of personal and group prayer, goals and objectives of Evangelization, forming and growing the Evangelization team, building up the church from within, social justice, personal stories from the street and some last thoughts on perseverance. Also, I have whole chapters devoted to goals 2 and 3 of the Bishops' document. There are ideas for meeting Goal 1 for bringing up the confidence and the knowledge of the people in the pews scattered throughout the pages which follow because you can't do anything without the support of the community you have and you need everyone to make your efforts work.

Jesus said before He ascended "Go and make disciples of all nations, baptizing them in the name of the Father and of the Son and of the Holy Spirit" (Matt 28:19). The call to mission did not die out with the apostles but is very much needed today. YOU are needed today. Will you answer God's call?

2

Prayer

So you are probably thinking still, "how does this apply to me?" How can I do something with this to build up the Church?

Here is the simple answer. Pray. Just pray.

How is God speaking with you? Learn to listen as God speaks, learn to recognize His movements and promptings in your heart and in your life. Use whatever prayer tools you feel comfortable with to build up your own relationship with God. Sometimes God uses other people. He uses books, the Bible, visions, inner locutions where you "hear" His voice. He can use smells to trigger thoughts or memories and give you things to consider. God is not limited in the way He can address you. It is up to you to figure that out. Each one of us is unique and also has unique needs as far as communicating with God. He knows this and He is capable and willing to work with you. You need to reach past what you are comfortable with to see where and how God is inviting you. It takes practice and lots and lots of prayer. You need the prayer as your basis for anything you do for Evangelization. It is still God's Church and it is up to Him how it will be led forward. And it is up to you to be the hands and the feet and sometimes that sore and aching back when you are in the trenches doing some really basic stuff that seems like it is all work and no pay off. God is the driver in all things. Are you willing to let Him take the wheel and guide you? What does God want to do for His Church? How does He want to use you as His instrument? I can tell you from experience that even if you think you have a good idea, if it doesn't have God's backing, it will flop. So, once again, prayer and discernment are so important to see where God's Spirit is really leading you, because by your willingness and openness, others will come to know God and be healed. Are you ready? No really ready? Prayer is the foundation that ties you to God and keeps you joyful.

Pope Francis says it best. "You don't want to look like you just swallowed vinegar." You want people to be able to see your joyful spirit. I will also say that if you don't pray constantly, it is very easy to get burned out and grumpy. Evangelization is not just a job that has to be done. It is our calling and our duty, but it needs to be done in a way that glorifies God. Our joyful witness to Jesus is the way God is glorified. Grumpy faces have the opposite effect.

I have also heard it said to "do it until you feel it." I'm not saying you should put on a phony smile. People know, they sense at a deep level, the difference between real and phony. As an evangelist, you always want to be authentic, real, present, personable, the face of Jesus in whatever situation. I once had an event that I went to. I was having an absolutely miserable day. I thought "O God, how can

I do this?" I did my set up (we'll talk more about that in a later chapter) and inhaled deeply. On my exhale, I prayed Jesus to cover me and fill me. I felt peace and was able to really smile again. It is not we who do the work, but God Himself, even through our weaknesses or maybe especially because of our weaknesses that His glory becomes manifest.

The example I just gave was a form of centering prayer. Because I had familiarity with this prayer type, it was easy for me to recall it and practice it in a very short span of time. Prayer is like a second skin. Usually though, I am in trouble and my prayer is "O God, O God, O God, O God!!!!!!!!!" as I look to God to get me out of some mess or other. Prayer doesn't stop once the team is established, or the Evangelization goal is met. It is a constant that you should put on and sink into to assist in all aspects of the Evangelization effort and, well, life in general.

This chapter will briefly go over several different prayer forms and types that will allow you to explore other avenues and will help expand your God awareness. Full books are written on each of these forms and this is just an introduction to you to open up possibilities that maybe you didn't know existed so that your prayer life can be deepened.

God doesn't need our prayer. He wants us to pray because as we do, we learn the heart and mind of God and hear His will for us. God knows that as a people we have a short attention span. When we make a practice of saying prayer, we keep our hearts turning to God and not to ourselves. Prayer then helps us to grow and keeps us on the right track, the track of God's will.

So let's begin with the prayers we are most comfortable with. Our Father, Hail Mary, Glory Be and the Mass. Yes, the Mass. Most people just take the Mass for granted. The Mass is the perfect prayer. We cover the readings of the Bible, the inspired Word of God. We recall our connection with the Jewish people with whom God made a lasting covenant that extends to us through Jesus' action in the world. We pray the words that Jesus gave us to pray in the Our Father. We receive Jesus' body and blood. At times, we experience the other sacraments as part of the Mass. We sing hymns of praise to God that mirror the voices of heaven, so that in all these things, heaven touches the earth. The Mass is the place where the fullness of God's love and mercy can be experienced. How many times do you take the Mass for granted and idly make a grocery list or worry about conversations you had or feelings others evoked in you instead of paying attention to the great mystery unfolding before you!? The Mass should be enjoyed and experienced fully with all the sights and the smells evoking memories and feelings of connectedness in us, evoking imagery of God's tender love for us. The Mass is the place when we can place all our cares before God and receive His benefits. We are strengthened for the Mission of spreading the faith and being God's witnesses. We have peace and love from God nurturing and nourishing us in our deepest selves. We are in intimate union with our

Prayer

Creator. We are laid bare before Him with all our failings and flaws, but still are communicated that immeasurable love from Him to us, which fills our hearts with joy, if we allow Him in. Mass then is that mountaintop of the Transfigured Jesus from which we are sent on our way. The apostles were not allowed to stay in the place of transfiguration but were called to go forth. We can fill up again and again at this place of refuge as food and strength for the journey. Mass and all its benefits, healing and joys is offered and available to us every day. We just need to avail ourselves of those opportunities and see them as times for spiritual growth and renewal and not just as a chore to get through to get on with the day. The Mass is the evangelist's greatest tool and comfort. We have communal prayer - the prayers of the community and our own needs presented as we pray together as one. We are tied together as a community of believers acknowledging our need and reliance on God. We know that we are not alone but that everyone around us also has concerns or worries and that together we can call upon God and ask Him to bless all of who are before Him. We are a family of believers and struggling children. Each one loved immensely by God, the Father who cares and provides for us.

Jesus taught us the Our Father prayer. How can God not pay attention when we pray this, since these are the words of His beloved Son? Do you rush through this prayer and not give it a thought, or do you savor each word as a gift from Jesus who poured Himself out for us? I once prayed this prayer over the span of two hours. I contemplated each word and its meaning. What does "our" mean? Our means for everyone, all of us who have been given the right and the privilege to call upon God, all of us here on earth who are tied to each other through God's grace and love for us. "Father" means male head of household, provider, teacher and model of what our behavior should be. What does having a good father mean? What is He trying to teach you? How is He leading you onward? You can take each word of this prayer and contemplate on the meaning and why it is significant. Forgive us as we forgive others. Now we have a little more difficult prayer. We are called to step out of our comfort zones to forgive others. If we don't forgive, nor shall we be forgiven when our time comes. Jesus told Mary Magdalen that her sins were forgiven because she loved much (Luke 7:47). Don't we want to receive the fullness of God's mercy? We are called to show that compassion first to others no matter how much they may have hurt us. Taking the time to go through the Our Father prayer like this, hopefully gives a better understanding of God's great love for us. The same method can be used to go through the other prayers that we all know.

Meditating on scripture is particularly good for doing the *lectio divina* method of prayer. The basic form of *lectio divina* is to put yourself into the scripture passage that is read, to become one of the characters and to allow the full extent of the experience to wash over you by reading the readings with the eyes of being a participant or an observer

Prayer

and letting God speak to you and touch your heart in that way. When I pray the Hail Mary prayer, I recall the words and the moment the Angel Gabriel appeared to Mary and announced Jesus' birth. In my meditation, sometimes I am Mary, other times just someone standing close to her. I experience all the emotions and thoughts she experienced by having an angel messenger of God appear to her, emotions of fear, unworthiness, awe of the Divine God, love for God, trust in His word, excitement, anticipation or knowing that something really big was about to happen and only God knew where it was going to lead because this event was beyond your understanding. Do I trust God's word enough to say yes unreservedly to what He is asking? Do I second guess what I think I know to be true and replace it with my own logical expectations? Am I really open to God's leading or am I just giving Him lip-service? Am I ready to say, lead me Lord because your servant is ready, or am I saying I only want to go so far and limit God's hand? Mary, help of sinners, pray for us, we really need your help. Help us as we struggle with our human failings and frailties. Help us as we journey into the unknown which is God's realm for building our trust and faith.

Give God a chance to answer your questions and thoughts. Spend some time with God in silence. If you have a conversation with someone, don't you give them a chance to speak when your turn is over? Prayer is the same thing. It is two-way communication not just from you to God. Listen, really listen to what God is trying to tell you. It won't always be something you want to hear but it will always be what you need. I find that when I have issues, or I want to vent or just spend time in silence away from the busyness of life that I go to Eucharistic Adoration where Jesus is truly present. He is SO available in that form, so near. My greatest joys and some of my ideas have come from those times when I am in adoration. Several different forms of prayer are included in this one. Contemplation of the face of Jesus present in the host species. Meditation on His body and blood poured out for all to wash the world clean. Centering prayer for listening to the word of God in your heart. Songs of praise and thanksgiving that bubble up for the good God has done for you and the joy in His presence. Prayers of sorrow and remorse for those times when you weren't the best you can be. Petitions for those in need. Thanksgiving prayers for answers received. In my mind, Eucharistic adoration is right next to the Mass as far as being a multi-faceted prayer type.

My husband does not get the fulfillment from adoration I do. He has found much more comfort in doing the Liturgy of the Hours. This is an old prayer form and is the prayer of the Church, the Divine Office. This prayer ties you in with people who are praying the same prayers all around the world so you are raising your voices as one praying the prayers of the church together even though you may be in the privacy of your own home. Like the Mass, you are all tied together by the common bond of this prayer form. I find this prayer very difficult and tedious. My mind starts to wander and I have difficulty focusing on it.

It is for this reason that we are so blessed in the Catholic church to have the varying prayer types and forms so that we can find the ones that are appealing and beneficial to our own needs and circumstances, that fill, uplift us and connect us to God. As stated previously, there are many books written on these varying prayer types. There are also instructional classes available with teachers who can guide you through some of the basics so you can make that prayer form your own and add it to your bag of tools. Above all, prayer is a way to connect you with God's heart. Pray with your heart and God will fill your heart with His words. Be near to Him and He will be near to you. Choose to make the sacrifice of your time in prayer and you will not be sorry you did. Prayer, your heartfelt and personal prayer, is the root of all Evangelization. Prayer helps you live your life as if you believe what it is you are saying. Evangelization is God's work. Don't expect to do it on your own with any success. Let God lead this dance. Prayer makes you available to follow the lead. Prayer gives you that deep, meaningful relationship with God that allows you to then help others explore their relationship with God, to plant or nurture that seed of faith in the other with love and gentleness and grounds you in hope, purpose and meaning.

An abundant prayer life also spurs you to want to share your love of Jesus with others. Prayer is the ever-present wellspring that is always available to fill you and strengthen you. It keeps you rooted in God and humble, so that you allow Him to do His work through you. Prayer helps you in your discouragement to lift you up again when you have felt the sting of rejection or failure. It is that balm of God's love to fix and to soothe your tired hearts.

I'm not telling you how but, in St. Paul's words, "Pray unceasingly" (Eph 6:18). Find your own prayer voice and style.

3
The Work of Evangelization

Evangelization is something each one of us is called to do as a result of our Baptism into Jesus. We have received the Good News. We have been made part of God's family, we are called forth to spread the good news to others. Our very mission as Church is to fill the whole world with God's message of love and peace and joy. Unfortunately, many Catholics believe that it's the priest's job or that it's the parish council's job, or it's a job that belongs to someone other than you. I was called to be a witness and so are you. Everything we do as Church can be viewed through the lens of Evangelization. Do you have a group of women who brings food to those who have surgery or are elderly, or are homeless? That is Evangelization. Do you have a ministry where knitters make hats or shawls for people with cancer? That is Evangelization. Do you help chop food or do clean-up for church suppers? That too is Evangelization. Do you spend time with the elderly and listen to them tell their stories or play cards with them or just visit? That too is Evangelization. Going out on the street is just a really small part of Evangelization. The truth is, Evangelization is more about connecting with people one on one and making them feel loved by God, special, appreciated and worthwhile. By our love we are known as Christians. Once people feel that individual acceptance by you, they are more likely to open up and allow you to talk about God and the good things God has done for you. Very little about Evangelization is being a great theologian. Sometimes those conversations come up. For the most part, it's about talking to people and making connections of trust. It's not about the numbers, it's about person to person trust and time. It's also about listening and making others feel that what they have to say is important to you. Their lives, their stories, their hurts and their joys, all of it. <u>Active</u> listening shows real compassion. When you meet people, either new in the church or on the street, it is very important to remember their names. If you remember their name and key things about them from the conversation you had, you are more likely to grow a connection with them. I knew a man who was absolutely amazing at this. He loved people and he loved to talk to people. If he was at a restaurant, he would immediately engage the server, find out their name, their age, what else they did, if they were in school etc. Then he would find a connection with them either from the school they were going to, the neighborhood they lived in, whether they know such and such a family in that neighborhood. Maybe he would even make an association based on their last name for someone he went to school with as their

The Work Of Evangelization

parent or grandparent. He made everyone he came in contact with feel immediately special and part of his world. The next time he would see them, he would continue the conversation as if they were his best friend. He really was amazing. I once went to a retreat and the question they asked was if you could invite two people to dinner, who would they be and why. My answer was Jesus, and this man. Jesus, to pick his brain, and this man who would keep the conversations going. Remembering people's names and truly listening to their needs, pain and concerns are more necessary than theological expertise when evangelizing.

I have heard people say that they can't evangelize for whatever reason - they don't feel worthy, they can't answer the tough questions, they don't know what the real teaching of the church is on any particular point. I ask you this. How difficult is it to acknowledge someone new in the church, to greet them with a smile and a warm welcome? That is Evangelization. Almost everyone can do that. A warm greeting acknowledges that the person is noticed and not just part of the woodwork. There is a couple I know who have been attending church for five years and no one said hello to them until my husband and I stopped and spoke with them after Mass. We had been in the parish three years and they preceded us. How sad is that? Don't we all like to be acknowledged, welcomed, greeted kindly and invited to be a part of whatever is taking place? Many people have already had bad experiences with the Catholic Church. Let's not add unwelcoming to the list of failings. Being welcoming to strangers is up to each and every one of us. It's not difficult and doesn't take a lot of time, practice or skill. No different from what you would say to someone on line at the grocery store or in any other public place. You are most likely already doing it, it's just a matter of extending your focus to the Church arena. Remember the words of the Beatitudes "I was a stranger and you welcomed me."

Here is something else you are also already doing but don't realize is part of Evangelization. You are probably praying for people for healing, financial situations, to return to the church or whatever other needs people may have. Let people know you are praying for them. There is a tremendous comfort in knowing that you are not struggling alone and that you matter enough to someone that they pray for you. I have heard it said that you shouldn't let people know you are praying for them because that's like tooting your own horn, that you already have your reward here on earth and you will miss out in heaven. My thinking is, let people know that we are connected to God through each other's prayers. Don't worry so much about your crown in heaven but help people with their spiritual hurdles on earth. Let those who don't feel like they belong or are struggling know that they are loved and cared about as individuals, not just a number to increase Mass attendance. Plant the seeds of hope which may take years to mature but could start with your words and prayers for them. Trust that God is using you in each moment for

The Work Of Evangelization

some good work. Love others by being who you are and using the talents and gifts that God gave you. That is the work of Evangelization.

Evangelization is not only about just paying attention to others while in church. It should also spill over into your every sphere of life. When I was working, I had this junky little image of the Lady of Guadalupe on my desk. It was a brown background with a white outline of the Blessed Mother that stood about three inches tall. Very cheap plastic. I might have paid $.50 for it. There it sat on my desk. I didn't have to let everyone in the office know I was religious, but this junky little statue was enough for people to come over to me and start talking or ask for prayer for whatever their needs were. I didn't have to wave my arms or take newspaper ads out or even announce things over the loud speaker. People just knew they could come talk to me. Another time, I was scooping ice cream at the local ice cream shop and had my head in the freezer and up to my elbows in ice cream. Someone said to me as I was in that awkward pose, "I can tell you are a Christian." "Why, yes I am," I answered. How would he have known? So it should be in all aspects of our lives. People should get the sense that we are so much connected with God that He hears us when we pray and that we have something that they too want to have. We really need to live our faith as if we believe that God is really present to us and to everyone else too. Therese Lisieux had it right I think. She said do the little things every day with love. You are blessed by God and each thing you do in the day is a job given to you specifically, by God, to do. How wonderful it is to serve God with a happy heart and joyful countenance in each moment of each day, knowing that each minute is a job given to you specifically! What a purpose and a meaning that gives to your life, that each minute grows God's kingdom in word and deed if you are open to His leading!

Here are a few more things that could easily be incorporated into building up the parish community. Many churches offer hospitality monthly or quarterly. For an interesting take on hospitality, you may be able to get one "group" within the parish to celebrate another "group." For example, you could have the college eligible teens put on a hospitality to celebrate those who retired in that year or vice versa. You could have the parish council celebrate the people in the parish who may have had new babies in the year. Or you could have the Faith Formation team and children do an event, like the Christmas pageant, for those who are in the nursing homes or in senior housing. In these ways, you are bringing groups together and celebrating each other as community and individual talents. I knew of a church who used to host a dinner for new members. What they would do is have one or two families who were long time members of the community host a pot luck or other dinner for a few new members of the parish. By doing that, new people were embraced, made to feel welcome and knew people in the church when they went. Host families were on a rotation so that all the expense

The Work Of Evangelization

did not fall on a few people and new members were all brought into the community.

How many saints have you read about who were considered too dumb for holy orders but were allowed to tend the animals or be a doorman. Within those places of humble trust and service of the Lord where they were, God used them to pray for and console others, such that hundreds came flocking to them, looking for their specific prayers. The truth is that we don't have the bigger picture but God does. We should find it exciting that God empowers us to build His kingdom in even the small ways we experience daily, in our normal lives, in our normal interactions with others. I have this eager expectation in each interpersonal encounter to watch as God's hand and will unfold. Sometimes I receive blessings, other times I help impart them, but I am never again the same because I have felt God's undeniable presence in that moment.

Another point to consider about Evangelization is that one plus one does not equal two. Where that is true in the mathematical sense, it is not so for the spiritual. On a good day you do the work to put on some event or activity and you hope that people will come, be enlivened by the experience and continue to grow in their faith journeys or even, better still, be moved to assist in your Evangelization efforts. Very rarely do things work out as planned. In the spiritual world, one plus one could be 16 where God blesses people in uncounted ways or one plus one could equal a half where the desired outcome you anticipated didn't happen but you hope that at least somebody was touched. It is very difficult to quantify the workings of the Spirit. It may take twenty years for the Spirit to come to fruition in a person's life. You just don't ever really know. This is where trust in God is important. If you have prayed God's guidance and support for your efforts, then trust that He continues to be at work even in circumstances which appear to not have gone well. Everything has a reason in His time. Even the things which don't seem to make sense to us or seem like failures have an impact. It is far better not to have solid expectations about your own desired outcomes for any given event but to do the best you can in any situation and then sit back and watch as God unfolds it before you. The more expectations you have, the more disappointed you are bound to be if things don't fit your predetermined mold. Allow yourself the joy of watching God's action unfold. It will always be interesting if you let Him in. Even when things don't proceed as planned, God gives you little graces which are affirmations of His presence and love for you. Be open to receive them and to recognize them when they come up. They are the little miracles that get you past the rough spots. I think that a large part of effective Evangelization is the ability to be flexible and to roll with the situations and think fast on your feet. If you are rigid and highly structured, this is probably not the ministry for you although, as with all things, some structure is necessary. Evangelization is more about flexibility and availability to God rather than planning. It is about recognizing windows of op-

The Work Of Evangelization

portunity and being aware enough and courageous enough to act on them when God prompt you to. It should bring you peace knowing you sit in God's will, ready and available for any interaction which might occur for the benefit of God's Kingdom. This becomes your "yes" to God. Evangelization is, above all else, an adventure of the possible in the present which you have the privilege of being part of. O happy day to be of service to God in even the smallest of tasks!

4
Building the Evangelization Team

You have a fire in your bones and you are gung-ho about going out and doing. Where do you begin? Go talk to your priest and get his input. It definitely will not be a success without his approval.

Personally, I'm not sure that a team is the right way to go. That sounds odd coming from me I realize. Here's my thinking. Some churches are really good at one or more of the aspects of Evangelization that were mentioned in the first chapter. They see everything they do as a part of their mission as Church. I would say that that type of environment probably doesn't need a dedicated team. Again though, each church is different with things that fit or work better in some than in others churches. There is no one right answer. Some parish councils do a really good job of using the lens of Evangelization for their efforts. Other places have an Evangelization team in name but the functions they do are those of a parish council. Two very different environments and church personalities. In another church, the men's group was the one that did all the outreach. If you are interested in Evangelization, you need to know a little of the way your church does business and then, tailor an Evangelization approach that will fit well in your parish. Maybe there is only one aspect of your parish that is lacking like adult faith faith formation. Or maybe you have a burning desire to see some more social justice activities going on. In any event, you need to spend some time in your parish, talking to people who are on the various committees and ministries and to the priest for their input. Evangelization efforts should not be done in a vacuum but really do need to impact every aspect of church life. It's a good thing to include the key groups early in your discussions and idea formulations. It is also important to ask that they pray for you and your efforts. It is equally important that other ministries understand you are not trying to take over, just maybe tweak the way things are done to enhance the perception of the recipients to be more inclusive and welcoming.

In the church that I call home, there was no team for Evangelization until I started one. They are a very spiritual group of people, just not very outgoing. I started the team with the idea of presenting other opportunities to help them grow in their faith and self-confidence (Goal 1 of the <u>Go and Make Disciples</u> Bishops' Document). It is out of this team that the street Evangelization efforts took shape. Street Evangelization is not something I had thought of, but here it was, packaged, ready and available. I will speak more on that in a later chapter. For now, I am going to continue down the road of building a team.

Most of the people I chose for the team were

Building The Evangelization Team

hand-picked by me. I knew they were joyful and energetic people who wanted to share their faith with others. I also ran an ad in the church bulletin and picked up a few people from there. We had a few meetings but most of our communication was done over the computer and email. We started praying, collectively and individually. We placed our petitions in the prayer book in the adoration chapel. We had charismatic groups pray over us and our efforts. We just immersed ourselves in prayer, remembering that it is God's Church and He will guide us and use us as He pleases. We did some brainstorming of ideas of what we thought we could accomplish. No idea was considered too stupid or insignificant. We tried to work with all of the ideas presented to build them up into something. We found that, after some discussion, certain ideas were let go and others were pursued. We developed a plan of action that seemed doable.

Try to limit the number of meetings you have. Meetings should be short and productive. Nobody wants to spend endless hours in meetings where the air is filled with useless blah blah blah. Don't have a meeting for the sake of having a meeting. We all have better things to do with our time. I have had 2 meetings with my local Evangelization team. We had our first meeting so everyone could get to know each other and brain storm ideas. Our second meeting occurred when we were ready to go out on the street and I showed everyone what we had purchased with our funds, how the set up would go and what we had for give-aways etc. All other communication is done via email where people can read it based on their schedules and are still be able to express themselves without being limited by place and time.

Another thing to consider is to have speakers or trainings offered during your meetings on Evangelization-specific topics. You could also do a question and answer session within the group. This way, the meetings are more interesting and all team members can be learning individually and about each other's strengths at the same time.

Because the Evangelization team is an overarching function for the entire parish, one of the most important things that you need to do is foster lines of communication between and among the ministries in the church and even within the team itself. Communication is the way to grow involvement and also defeat the rise of cliques and potential negative feelings that could occur. It is important to build trust relationships within the parish and with those you minister to, which is why communication is so important. Knowing that Satan wants to block your efforts at every turn, you need to keep vigilant about your own personal feelings and emotions and nip them in the bud when they surface. That's why, too, prayer is such an integral part of any Evangelization effort because you all remain in God's covering protection. As an Evangelist, you are on the front lines of the battle and therefore, most likely to be attacked, distracted or beset with discouragement because Satan does not want you to succeed.

Building The Evangelization Team

Cover yourselves and your work in God's mighty power through prayer.

Within The Team Communication

Be aware of people's attitudes and feelings. If someone was perky but is now becoming reclusive, find out what is wrong. Maybe they have personal issues and aren't able to keep their commitments or maybe there was an issue of "he said she said" on the team that is causing some latent hostility. Be gentle but get to the bottom of things and let them know that they are not alone and that you and others are praying for them. Some people are afraid to say anything for fear of losing their spot on the team. Reassure them that their place is safe. Do whatever it takes to continuously foster good relations and keep the team cohesive. Team building exercises and yearly retreats are a good way to keep good friendships and relationships. Above all else, don't let things fester until they blow up. Resolve whatever issues there are quickly. It's the same advice you would give to a married couple. In a sense, you are married. You are the group God has called forth to work together and you need to make it work. Avoid gossip in the parking lot or afterwards on the phone or email. Avoid the snickering and the "he said she said" game. Have peace in your hearts toward each other. Be conduits of God's love so He can work through you for the good of all the entire church community. Remember that it is not about you but about how God is using you for the collective good you can do together.

Within The Parish Communication

There is a good chance that you will encounter negativity from the people in the parish when you start an Evangelization effort. People tend to guard their positions fiercely. As an over-arching function, people may see you as trying to encroach on their "spot." You could run into people who say that they have never done that before and are resistant to any changes you could propose. A good axiom to consider is "if you keep doing the same thing you've always done, then, you're going to get the same results." Our churches are shrinking and change is an important way to try to renew church life. In doing the same thing, why would you expect different results? Parish cliques want to keep things the same. They are very hard to eradicate because the thinking behind the behavior remains the same. You can try doing whole parish missions or retreats for ministry leaders with some success in order to let them know what Evangelization is or is not. These negative behaviors and characteristics are extremely difficult to overcome. Ministry leaders could also be invited to participate in the Evangelization meetings so they know that you are not trying to stomp on their efforts but are trying to create an integrated approach. Not only do you have to build trust relationships within the team but with the rest of the parish as well. If you don't have buy-in from the parish community, your efforts are bound to fail. Hopefully, your efforts won't be deliberately sabotaged, but you won't get support either which will be a negative spiral of failure then discouragement which will cause infighting among you and the eventual death of your group. Satan wins because you are tied and can do nothing.

If you can get ministry leaders on board with what you are doing, you are also more likely to get new recruits for your efforts, since part of being on a team is to keep building it up and getting new recruits, fresh blood and new ideas. Perhaps strong resistance is also God's way of showing you that you may need to change tactics and He's got another plan for you all. Be open and above board with all the church leadership. Be gentle and welcoming of their hesitant responses. Perhaps they too have had negative experiences with various groups and are expecting the same from you. Ask God to guide you along the way and don't get discouraged. All parishioners and ministry members need to be aware that everything you all do is for the greater good of the entire community and that no one group works in a vacuum and that you need each other in order to grow.

Communication With Those Ministered To

People can tell right away when you are insincere or lying. Again, you need to build trust and be as open as possible about what you are doing and why you are there. If someone asks you a question you don't know the answer to, be honest. Honesty, humility and a servant's attitude are the best ways to build people's trust. If you say you are going to do something like call or get them information or whatever, be sure to follow-up and get it to them. I can't tell you how many times I have had to chase someone down to get something they promised to give me. Then everyone gets annoyed because you look irresponsible and like you are making up stories or worse, serving your own needs or people will get discouraged and just not come back. A bad taste will be left in their mouths about you and you will be considered a hypocrite. None of these are the outcomes you were looking for. Really bad form.

I think that Evangelization efforts can be broken down to three "Cs" - Commitment, Community and Communication. And of course, prayer. Being persistent in your commitments, building the entire church community and communicating openly are important aspects to keep before you.

With the background on what we did, I'd like to offer some thoughts.

1. Talk to people and invite them to come join your efforts. You are more likely to get results with a personal invitation to someone.

2. Let people know that their ideas are welcome and that they won't be made fun of for anything off-the-wall that they may present. People need to feel safe before they express any ideas and confident that they are heard. If the idea is not

one that is workable at that point in time, maybe it could be tabled for later or reworked to a slightly different approach.

3. Ideas don't belong to the individual but become the property of the Holy Spirit to use and direct as He sees fit. Too often, people hold onto their ideas with a choke hold and do not let the light of the Holy Spirit in to mold it according to His plans. It is not our Church but God's. God knows how best to use us to bring about His purposes. We need to let Him. To some people He gives ideas, to others the means and the way to carry them forward. We need each other and we need to be able to work together. Each one of us is given a small piece of the puzzle that we form into a complete picture with our willingness and obedience to God. We are given different giftings to help the pieces work and flow together. Remember, God has hand-picked each of you to be in that time, that place, to work together for His purpose. The individual gifts will all come into play somewhere down the road. Be open to go where and how the Holy Spirit leads, sometimes on really short notice!

4. Prayer, prayer and more prayer. Pray for each other, pray for God's instruction and guidance. Pray for the hearts that will be reached because of your collective efforts. Be humble and listen to what God wants. Don't just perfunctorily say a prayer at the beginning of any meeting. Pray with the will of humble obedience and joyful

expectation that your prayer will be answered with something that will work best for you and your group.

5. Learn what each one brings to the table, both strengths and weaknesses so that each person can best be put to use by employing the gifts God gave them. As you get comfortable with each other, you may want to also try to grow in new areas where you hadn't considered before. You can partner with someone who has the talent set you would like to learn. Just because we are evangelizing others doesn't mean that we stop growing. Growth and new experiences are part of what keeps us fresh, joyful and hopeful.

6. Be careful about gossip. Satan wants nothing more than to undermine your efforts. He doesn't want God to be known or people's hearts to be opened. As soon as you form your group, be prepared for Satan's attacks to begin. Squabbles within the group, power struggles, gossip and back stabbing are all ways he works against you. You may also find yourselves having health issues or family having health issues that require your attention. There are any number of things that will seem like "coincidences" that will prevent you from doing the work God has set for you. Again pray for God's help in these trials. Pray for His angels to protect you. They will. Have faith. Our God is faithful. Trust Him and that good will come out of your temptations and trials. The St. Michael the Archangel prayer is a powerful protection for you.

Building The Evangelization Team

7. Some people really are poisonous. They may profess that they are free spirits or open to new things but really are close-minded and very likely the first to gossip. These people need to be let go. It's not always easy for a team or a leader to make that decision but if someone is doing more harm than good with their negative attitudes, they need to be told that the Evangelization team is not for them. These self-titled "free spirits" could also lead you away from Church teaching into non-Catholic areas and really do damage with what you are trying to do with increasing people's knowledge and understanding of the Faith. Other people may come to the realization that Evangelization is not for them on their own and fall away. It is part of the ebb and flow of life and change. God provides and protects. He changes and shifts according to what He wills.

8. Pray some more.

In our next chapter we will look at what to do once you have the team.

5

Setting Goals and Objectives

I knew a church who said they wanted to do Evangelization but they didn't do anything. Each month at the team meeting, they would go over the goals and the objectives for doing Evangelization, going over every detail of the wording to make sure it was right before they would attempt to do something. Any enthusiasm for Evangelization was long lost in the tedium of making it look good on paper. New members were told that there would be things to do later on. I tell you that the new members all fell away because that promise of things to do 'someday' just seemed too far off. We are told not to be hearers of the word but doers (James 1:22). In fact, the last words we hear at Mass each week are "go and" do, accomplish, teach, preach, be brave but DO something!

Here is my easy to follow goal: (Matt 28:19) "Go therefore and teach all nations baptizing them in the name of the Father and of the Son and of the Holy Spirit." We are also told not to worry about what we are to say or how we will get there for it will be God who speaks through us (Matt 10:19-

20). We need to be available and ready to move. It's not about making it look good on paper. Do something, even if it is wrong. Pray, listen and then do. Pray, reassess, change course and do. Pray and do are the operative words.

So you're thinking of doing an international night of food, dress and multicultural activities. You might be thinking that this is a party not an Evangelization activity. Building community and friendships is always a good way to start and learning to trust each other. There are also multiple layers of assistance that would be needed to do an event like this. You yourself may not have the tools to plan and organize the event from start to finish, but trust that God has someone in your midst who would be able to. Make it known in the parish bulletin, on the church bulletin board and even in the local papers what your plan is. Trust God to move hearts. People will come forward with the gifts that you need.

I was once doing a church supper. I started cooking early in the day. It was a staff of me and, oh yeah, me. I had a knock on the back door around 3pm. A woman from a neighboring church had seen the sign that we were going to have a dinner and she came over to help. Wow! She knew her way around the kitchen and the overwhelming task was made a lot smaller with her presence there with me. She was an answer to a prayer I didn't even know I prayed! I'm not saying to leave everything up to chance. What I'm saying is that things will work out. You will get what you need and you will

Setting Goals And Objectives

get it done. Many of you will say, "I'm not good at this or that, I could never do that Evangelization stuff." That woman was doing the work of Evangelization with me by slicing onions. For any event you do, there is set up and clean up and possibly food prep or service, garbage removal or any number of other small tasks that can be done. If each person takes on a small role, the entire event gets moved along. We are not called to do big things but the little things that we can and to work as a community of believers, looking out for each other. All of a sudden that insurmountable task of putting on such an event becomes much smaller because there are more hands to help. As Church, we are all called to evangelize in the small ways we can. People need to be encouraged to courageously step forward.

Many times there are cliques in the church. Anyone who is anyone will be with this or that group while the rest of us are left out. Whether the perceived clique is real or not, the fact remains that those doing the work get tired of being the ones to take things on time and again. There is no room for snobbishness in God's Church. We need to show our love and compassion to others and that begins in the church home. Forgiveness, acceptance, love and prayer are at the heart of all real ministry within the church. We also have a responsibility to pray for our own needs and growth so that God can make us more pliable and remove anything that hampers His will and direction. We need to keep vigilant, to work on those failings that He exposes about us. We need to continue to grow so we can offer ourselves up to be continuously used by Him.

Goals are important. You need to set goals which are realistic and attainable and you need to be able to measure your success somehow. If you set a goal of going out on the street to evangelize 6 times in this year, at the end of the year you can look back and see whether you made that goal. Did you go 6 times, did you go fewer times, did you exceed the goal and go more times? If you went fewer times, the reasons why need to be ascertained. If you went more times, great! Goals in themselves don't have to be complicated. They need to give you enough information to work with to assess your progress and give you positive feedback and encouragement for your continued efforts. I would warn you against making goals of increasing numbers of participants in any event. People, in general, tend to be in a state of flux. Couple that with being in a highly mobile society where you are not bound by parish boundaries and have the option of going to pretty much any church you can drive to in order to participate in their activities. More useful than numbers of participants would be a review of program evaluations to see where things could be improved. It is always important to do the after-event assessment to go over lessons learned, things that need improvement, requests or suggestions people had, etc.

Here is one example goal and objective setting and measurement:

Setting Goals And Objectives

Goal: To offer **four** Adult Faith classes of various types throughout the year.

Objective 1:(how you are going to get to your goal) Offer a small group session on the Eucharist

Objective 2: Have a speaker come in to do a mission for the church

Objective 3: Have a local group or artist come in to do a performance on the saints or the Passion of Jesus.

Objective 4: Offer a retreat on prayer.

This example illustrates an easy-to-measure evaluation process. Did you do what you set out to do? Yes or no? No church function should ever be about the numbers. It's up to God to bring people in and to move in their hearts. Just because someone shows up to one thing and not others doesn't mean they are not interested. You need to be consistent in what you offer to make it interesting and inviting to those who may be coming, both from your local church and from afar. I was once part of an Adult Faith Formation team in a church. We started out our process by asking parishioners what they wanted to see or participate in. The Needs Assessment we did at that time can be found in Appendix C. Based on their replies, we offered speakers each month on the topics they expressed interest in. We had already planned on having a Muslim Imam come in when 9/11 happened. People were angry and were venting at him when they showed up. He answered all their questions patiently. At the end of the evening, tempers had noticeably cooled and the people who attended had better understanding of Muslim faith than when they first arrived.

Getting back to goals. Keep them simple and doable based on the resources you have available. Lofty goal setting will end up being confusing and could potentially be discouraging if they are poorly understood, poorly executed and poorly attended. Successful activities spur more encouragement and cause creativity to blossom. Successful events also encourage other people to join in.

Here are some more thoughts:

1. Don't make a 10-year plan.

2. Start small and do one or two small things to get the ball rolling and the creativity flowing. As soon as possible after an event, go over things you learned or ideas you came up with that occurred to you while the event was taking place while it is still fresh in your mind. Start making plans for a future activity or event. Some events take longer to plan than others or are more involved. Leave yourself some planning room. A successful event will spur the creativity and will lead to something else. God is the author of all ideas. Trust Him.

3. Not all events, even though well-planned, will be a success. Don't be afraid to try. Maybe it was the wrong audience or the wrong timing or there was something else causing a blockage to

Setting Goals And Objectives

your event. Either way, even failures are lessons waiting to be learned. Maybe you need to go in a different direction, or maybe you need to explore a different type of event. I once had someone come to the church and present a one man play on the life of St. Paul. It was well advertised and we offered free dinner after Mass. Twenty-eight people showed up. There was a huge snow storm that night and people were afraid to venture out. Those who came really enjoyed the performance but the weather was just not something we had planned for. Next time, we know not to do something in February during the coldest and snowiest winter on record. Who would have known? Another time, I tried to start a youth ministry group. I had two kids show up. I was definitely upset about that one because I thought for sure that that was God's will for me. I did learn some lessons, the most important one being that large events need to have a prayer covering from a good portion of the members of the church in order for it to be successful. It also gave the Evangelization team a chance to build up together as a team. I also learned that I needed to trust my instincts and the stirrings of the Holy Spirit within my heart. Definitely valuable in the long run!

Does that mean I will stop trying? NO! If you experience failure, pick yourselves up, dust yourselves off and go back to the prayer board. Retain that sense of hopefulness that got you started on this path in the first place. Not always easy, I'll grant you, but definitely worth it in the long run. Maybe it was just a learning experience for your team, a growing point that you can take with you in the future. Trust God. Pray. God is still in control. Take a deep breath and smile. All will be well.

4. Don't be afraid to try again. Keep those ideas coming. Perseverance, elbow grease, and faith can make all things new in time.

5. Oh yeah, did I mention prayer?

6

Event Planning

I am including what I initially intended to be a checklist, but has turned into a chapter. There will be one example of a checklist I used when we had a speaker come in. I am including this information because sometimes people don't know where to begin in planning something. I hope this chapter will be useful to you to get started. I have tried to be as thorough as possible, but there could still be some things I missed. If you find that this checklist does not meet your needs and you are stuck, please feel free to email me at info@fishersonthestreet.org and I will be happy to assist you and to answer your questions. Also, I have seen whole books written on this very subject. I have included this section here as a get-you-started tool.

Identify your target audience and address those particular circumstances. A wine and cheese gathering is not the same as a coffee hour after Mass. They are two very different groups with different atmospheres. It's important to set a clear expectation of who will be the participants in this event and what the event is trying to do. Decide early on what the focus of the event will be. Will it be food for a social setting and a speaker invited in while people are eating or will it be the speaker as the focal point with the food as a secondary. All these decisions need to be made in the beginning by the planning team. Appropriate permission should be obtained in the planning process to determine what the limitations might be or even what the pastor is comfortable in doing.

As you get things going, I recommend keeping a folder with contact information and other pertinent information all together. You may want to have separate folders by function, as well, if that works better for you. I tend to keep things all together in one folder so that I can easily find things and that they don't get confused with whatever other project I have going on simultaneously. This chapter will have some of the key things to consider and decide upon as you plan and build your event.

Food

Decide in the planning stages if your event will have food or not. Also, make the determination ahead of time whether there will be a full meal or just refreshments of sorts. I am including everything to do with food. Some things may not apply to what you are planning. As a side thought though, food is always a good way to bring people in and bring people together.

Discuss ahead of time if you are doing a full meal, who is bringing what or will it be catered. If it is being catered, discuss also the cost limits per person for the number of participants you anticipate hav-

Event Planning

ing. Keep the caterer's name, phone number, email and other contact information, quote and what that will include handy. It will be useful to have this information when presenting to your governing church approval body. You could also decide to do a pot luck supper or a light soup and salad type supper. Here are things to consider if an in-house meal is the route you choose. Are there enough outlets and extension cords for the crock pots? How will you determine what people are bringing? Who is your target audience for the particular event? How many people are expected? Are you going to do a sign up or is there a RSVP deadline? Will adding people significantly change your catering cost?

How will the food be served – on paper plates or church dishes or will the caterer provide dishes as well? Think about serving utensils, napkins, cups and the other things you need to have when serving food. Many times serving utensils are an afterthought and people run around last minute trying to find something to serve with. Lastly, it is important to ensure that you have adequate garbage cans and bags close by. For larger events, you will also need to ensure that the cans are emptied regularly. Which brings up another point. Who is going to help with the set up or clean up prior to the event, during and after. I will speak more on this in the section on volunteers.

What will you do for beverages? Coffee? Other drinks? Bottled water? If you choose to have coffee (regular and decaffeinated), you also need to have creamer, sugar, non-sugar sweetener and other coffee accompaniments like stirrers, filters and garbage close by. If you offer hot tea or hot chocolate, then you will also need a way to make hot water, have tea bags and hot chocolate packets available. Also important to know is how to turn on the coffee pot and if it needs to be turned on by the breaker and how long it takes for the water to heat up. Someone among the volunteers should have a working understanding of how the coffee pot works. I once did a morning session and started a pot of coffee and ended up with cold coffee, an overflow and a really big mess. There I was rushing to get things done and had this big mess to clean up. I know now I should have checked this out ahead of time and allowed for extra time to get things ready. It's really hard to present yourself with grace and composure and look like you know what you are doing when the coffee pot is overflowing. I now know better and ask someone else to do the coffee.

If you are considering doing refreshments only, consider who is bringing what or will pre-made cookies or hors d'oeuvres be purchased. You could choose to do finger foods as well. Ensure there are adequate and appropriate beverages.

If you decide to do a breakfast, the processes are very similar.

Electricity/Lighting

If you are doing something inside the church itself, that is far more involved electrically than most halls. Someone who is familiar with the lighting in the church, like the sacristan, should be asked to assist for the event or to instruct someone in all the lighting possibilities.

If you are having a speaker address your congregation, proper microphone function becomes necessary to coordinate as well.

Also, you will need to find out ahead of time if you need to turn anything on like breakers to activate the outlets. This also means turning them off when you leave.

Facilities

When you are planning to do any event, including street Evangelization, it is a good idea to scope out the area ahead of time. Make sure you and your team know the area and exact location of where you are to meet. Going there ahead of time will let you know what parameters you will be working with regarding size, accessibility, parking, facilities like restrooms, location and how to turn on and off the heat or the air conditioning, or even barbecue grills etc. Make careful notes of what is available and what is not available. Maybe you will need electricity. Are there outlets, are they on and available to use? Will you need lighting? Or permission? Make notes of everything so that your team can plan appropriately. Questions will come up as you go. The more prepared you are, the smoother the event will go for you. Our Street Evangelization team made that mistake when we went to the Tulip Festival. My husband and half of the team couldn't find me because I hadn't done the leg work ahead of time. I'll talk more about that in a later chapter.

Are you having the event on Church grounds or someplace else? You need to have a good idea in mind of what you want to do before you decide on the facility. You can't have a bazaar with rides in the church basement. You need to plan according to the facilities you have available or branch out to other locations if you want to do bigger things. Keep in mind though, people don't like to leave their home parish. If you are planning an event off-site someplace, you are less likely to have a large portion of the parish attend. That's just the way people are. They are comfortable in their own space and more likely to attend something in familiar surroundings. It is not about the event but about bringing people together as a community.

What you need for facilities varies by event. Have an idea ahead of time of what you would like to see then determine whether you need tables and chairs moved or removed, do you need a podium, do you want to arrange furniture in a circle to make it more welcoming. A circle arrangement works for a group of no more than 15. Semi circles work for bigger groups. Also consider if this is a function where people will need to take notes, like a Bible study in which tables might be helpful. Do you have volunteers for set up and clean up? As your group discusses the flow of the event, this section on facilities is really where you determine how activities will occur and the space factors needed. Also consider whether you want to decorate with

Event Planning

a particular theme, or maybe just have tablecloths. You don't want to make extra work for yourselves if you don't need to but you want to make the area inviting and welcoming at the same time. As always, you do the best you can with the space and the materials you have available.

Volunteers And Communication

You can't do things alone and need to request help for some of these behind the scenes things. Your function will be primarily oversight since you will have the main idea of how things should flow. You also need to be ready to put out any fires the day before or the day of the event, like the overflowing coffee pot, because no matter how well you plan, something will always happen that is not in the plan. Someone may fall, supplies may not show up, the cake falls on the floor at the last minute because the table broke, etc. You can put your hands to any of the tasks but make sure you are available to answer last minute questions too. This is why volunteers are so important, whether or not they are part of your team. People generally want to help and want to be given direction. As the coordinator, you should not be shy about asking for specific tasks or giving clear direction of what needs to be done. Put announcements in your bulletin, ask the priest to talk it up during Mass, or maybe he'll even allow you to speak in front of the congregation. Don't wait until last minute but start recruiting weeks ahead of time. Let people know that this event is coming up and that help is needed. I did an event that needed 40 volunteers to ensure that everything went smoothly. I came up with creative ways to get people to help. I told them that their tickets were free for the talk if they helped. For the particular event, tickets were $25 which included lunch. All my volunteers got a free lunch and a free admission to the talk and parking in the parking lot closest to the church in the inner city where parking was scarce. This tactic ensured I had what I needed for help. Keep a good record of names, phone numbers and what they are willing to do and the hours they are available when you make your volunteer list.

When you are working with volunteers, be specific about the tasks they are to perform. A nebulous "you will be doing something but I'm not sure what" approach does not inspire confidence that you know what you are doing, nor does it peak their interest. When I did the speaker event, I called a meeting about a week ahead of time and gave everyone their assignments. I had ticket takers and greeters, parking attendants and food staff. I separated everyone by their function and dealt with them individually. When they were done they could leave and I addressed the next group. No one had to hear what another group was doing. I was specific on who was doing what and what their time involvement would be. The day ran longer than expected and was blistering hot, and the air conditioning stopped working but they all were troopers and kept to their posi-

Event Planning

tions even though, with all the unexpected issues, it turned out to be far longer and more difficult than we envisioned.

Another thing to consider for the volunteers is to get them name badges that set them apart from regular participants. For the event I have been talking about, I made bright orange tags that could be easily seen to set them apart. I included my cell phone number on the back of everyone's volunteer tag in case they needed to get a hold of me.

Lastly, you need to thank the volunteers afterwards for helping. I couldn't do a gift card because I had forty people, so I opted to run an ad in the bulletin with my deepest appreciation. You could do small gift cards to the local store, or even do a volunteer evening for refreshments where you let them know how it all went. Be effusive in your praise because you are more likely to get their help next time you need it. I did a pot luck supper one time. It was slated to start at 6:30pm. I had one of my previous volunteers show up at 5:30pm. In my usual grace and style, I told her the supper wasn't starting until 6:30 ('so what was she doing there?' I thought, since I wasn't used to people helping out)? She said, I knew you were doing this so I came to help set up. Wow! You could have knocked me over with a feather at that point. What that told me was that she felt needed and useful and liked working with me. She brought friends with her too! You can never be too grateful to your volunteers.

Communication lines also need to be clear. We all made several mistakes at the Tulip Festival and the Flag Day parade which I will point out. The full story of the Tulip Festival is in a later chapter.

• I didn't know how to work my phone.

• I wasn't aware that my phone was on vibrate not ring.

• Not everyone had a way to communicate as they were looking for us, that's why my husband couldn't get a hold of me to see where I was.

• Messages left on home answering machines were not checked before setting out. Even though I had called ahead of time to cancel a Flag Day event, one of the other team members never got that message because she went straight from one activity to another and then ended up getting stuck in the parade without the rest of us present with her as support.

As a result, we now know that we need to make sure that everyone was able to check either email or phone messages. I assured everyone that I would always communicate with them any changes but they needed to check on their end too. Communication is a two-way street and works if both/all parties participate.

Permissions

Another thing that is important before you put on any event is to make sure you have the permissions from the appropriate people. Permissions need to be obtained at all levels. The parish priest for parish-

Event Planning

wide events. The local zoning board, police department and city mayor for outdoor festivals off parish grounds. It is a good idea to check with them for events even on parish grounds to determine if there could be any restrictions. If you are doing street Evangelization, you also need to get permissions from the airports, park authorities, city officials of the towns and locations where you wish to evangelize in order to ensure that you have free access to passersby and will not be troubled by authorities as you do your work. Remember also to be respectful of their decisions. They have rules to follow too and don't need to be the brunt of your frustrations. You want to evangelize by your good spirit and cooperative attitude as well as your words. You don't know but where a seed could be planted by your attitude. Negative seeds could be planted as well. For that reason, it is important to have a joyful and happy attitude in all your dealings. You can easily become burnt out or bitter. Let prayer be your shield to help keep your joy. Remember too that God Himself will give you the words to say. Jesus promised it but you need to do your part too by keeping close to Him through prayer. I can't stress prayer enough because ultimately, it is not our work but God's work through us.

This is something that needs to be addressed early on in the process. Not only do you need to get permission from your parish priest, if you are doing something larger, even on the Church grounds, you may need to get the city or local authorities to give you clearance. Each town or area has different restrictions regarding assembly of persons. Most likely they will tell you to go ahead and that they don't need to be involved. In the off chance that they do, you will have covered this ahead of time and ensure there are no issues the day of the event. When I had the speaker come in, I also contacted the local EMTs to make sure they would be available in the event something happened the day of the event. I was thinking heat-related since it was going to be so hot. They told me they would hang out by the church. Wouldn't you know it. As soon as they left, we had a woman fall down the stairs. Fortunately, I also had a mental list of the medical professionals we had coming and was able to connect them with her fairly quickly. She was treated and all was well.

If you are planning on serving alcohol at the event, you need to obtain a liquor license which may be a "per event" license. Please, please, please do not have the youth ministry serving at an event where there is any type of alcohol. That would be a really bad mix. As church, we are called upon to protect our young people. Even in convenience stores and restaurants people under 18 years of age cannot sell or serve alcohol. It is the law. Especially in a time when the Church is under so much scrutiny, this is one area where potential problems could and should be avoided.

Date On Calendar

Once you get the permissions and all the parties involved agree on a date, it's important to get the date on the Church calendar. This is a necessary step in or-

Event Planning

der to start your marketing efforts. You, ideally, want several weeks prior to the event to start announcing it, in the bulletin, in the local papers, to other churches etc. You can make posters and hang them up at the doors of the church. Your marketing and posters are only limited by what your priest allows and your creativity. Colorful posters may require some financial expenditure if you do not have the tools available on site. Since God always provides, there is usually someone who has some design skills who may be able to assist in the creation of your advertising materials.

Some local stores may allow you to advertise your activity. We have posted flyers at the local Catholic supply store. We are blessed to have a Catholic radio station in the area who ran ads for us on the air. We also advertised in the local Catholic newspaper. Not all events would necessitate going to these lengths, but because we had a well-known speaker coming to the area, we wanted to reach as many people as possible.

Another thing to consider when you are doing your marketing is to have printed up programs for the day of the event, or event flyers, and also tickets for printing. It's usually cheaper to print tickets in house than to have them done professionally. The perforated card stock is cheap and available online.

Finances And Payment Schedule

Determine early on what your budget is for the event and what types of things will need to be purchased or rented ahead of time or the day of, and how these things will be paid for. Will you make the arrangements and the office staff will pay or will they cut you a check and tell you to go pick it up and pay when you get there, or will they give you the church credit card? It all depends on how your office staff are comfortable doing business. These things need to be worked out early in the process so there is no confusion later on. Ideally, your proposal would include cost for the speaker, airfare, hotel, if appropriate, food costs and supply costs so the priest and office staff know what to expect. Ticket pricing should then be set to recoup some or all of the expenses, but the major outlay for these items will come prior to the event taking place. For that reason, it is important for the church to be able to set aside the money far enough ahead. Again, there are always unexpected costs that come up, but hopefully you will have accounted for the big ticket items.

Pick up schedule

It is important to determine ahead of time who is picking up what, whether it's paper goods, decorations, food or refreshments, or the speaker from the airport. You can't do it all. This is where your volunteers are vital. Work the pick-up schedule into your volunteer meeting. Put down contact information for those doing the pick-ups and the people they will be interacting with to ensure adequate communication lines and decrease potential problems. Make sure also that everyone has a clear way of getting in touch with you.

Event Planning

Supplies

Although churches usually keep supplies and extra things on hand, it's a good thing to go over what you think you may need before the event to ensure that it is there and available for you to use. We did a soup dinner recently. There were no "chubby" soup cups, which were the priest's preference, or soup spoons available. The office staff ordered them and they were ready and available a few days prior to the event. Nobody thinks of toilet paper. If you are doing a large event, your bathroom facilities will be used more than usual. You need to plan for extra restroom supplies, including toilet paper, soap and paper towels, when you are taking stock of your paper goods. You also need to set up garbage cans and ensure that they are emptied periodically on the day of. That could be a task for one of the volunteers to keep an eye on. Your job is to ensure that there are sufficient cans and bags available throughout the day, both in the bathrooms and the food areas.

Knowing what is available is only half the job. How to find everything you are looking for and ensuring that you have the key to the locked storage facility is very important for the day of the event. Having appropriate keys to the store room or to the bathroom are things that need to be worked out with the office staff ahead of time.

You need paper goods for whatever food you are serving. You also need to know where the coffee pot is and whether there are sufficient coffee supplies like coffee, filters, sugar, creamer, stirrers, etc. Tea bags or hot chocolate, if you so choose, as well. And again, garbage bags and cans. People are usually good about cleaning as they go but you need to provide adequate garbage collection receptacles. An event could take a sour turn if the garbage area looks uncared for and unattended. It would also be useful to know where to take the full garbage bags for those assisting and if a key is needed to access the area.

Parking

Being part of an inner city church, parking is at a premium. That's why I was able to bribe my volunteers with parking. I requested barricades from the City to block off the parking lot to random people. Those who had parking passes issued by me ahead of time were allowed to park in the lot. The parking attendants also directed the participants to parking spots within the lot so we could fit more people in. And they had the list of names and plate numbers of all the people on the "approved" list. In rural churches, parking may not be such an issue. If you are looking at doing an event at a different location, you also need to assess parking as one of your facilities criteria you look for. Inadequate parking generally makes for grumpy attendees.

Prayer

Since you are putting on a Catholic event, you should also consider incorporating prayer as part

Event Planning

of the day. It could be a retreat day which starts and ends with a Mass. It could also be a brief prayerful reflection before other activities take place. You could choose to do prayer with the planning team or incorporate a wider audience. It is probably advisable to consider some element of prayer. Prayer is the universal uniter. If you are doing a short prayer service to begin or even throughout the day, you need to consider setting the atmosphere with decorative and meaningful throws, or other decorations. Candles, if they are allowed in your church, are always a good representation of Christ being the light of the world. Incense, holy water, a Bible with select passages marked ahead of time would also be helpful. If you are having someone do readings or assist with the presentation, they need to have their parts ahead of time so they can practice and polish how they would present. A little thought and effort in this regard can easily set the tone for the event as one of peaceful anticipation and participation with the workings of the Holy Spirit guiding how the day unfolds. You can also choose not to do an in-depth prayer but a simple prayer before a community meal. Choosing to do a prayerful interlude is one of the items that should be determined in your planning phase.

Looking back on what I wrote here, it could be intimidating. Think of a church event as a family Thanksgiving gathering but on a bigger scale. The same thoughts and planning processes are involved just in a different location and for the church family. Take a deep breath. Don't be afraid to ask for help. Rope in family, friends and favors if need be. It will all work out with prayer and a little planning. And just maybe, there will be a comical interlude that you can laugh about afterwards although it may seem catastrophic at the time. Nobody is perfect, so just do the best you can in any situation and trust God to fill in the rest. Happy eventing!

7

Limiting Factors

In this chapter I'm going to talk about the things that nobody wants to admit but are part of our human experience as human beings, and that is Limiting Factors. What do I mean when I say limiting factors? Just this. The things that limit your ability to achieve the goals you have set. These can take many forms and I will go through the most common ones like the relationship with the parish priest, money and budget considerations, people strengths and weaknesses and time.

The *priest* in the parish is the one who has the oversight responsibility for seeing that the parish functions, that bills are paid, programs are met as he and the bishop envision and that the roof doesn't fall down on people's heads. In some cases, the priest will delegate some of these functions but his oversight into these situations remains, because ultimately he is accountable to the local Bishop for the pastoral needs of the people. The physical building falls under this because if people are being rained on during Mass, they are less likely to be paying attention to the mystery taking place in the Mass itself. Because all these things are the priest's concern, he is less likely to take on another ministry like Evangelization where he perceives that it could be extra work for him. Evangelization should be the central point, other than the Mass, of why we are church. We are strengthened by the food of the Eucharist and the presence of Jesus and we are called forth to proclaim the gospel to others. Every ministry in the parish needs to be looked at with the critical eye of Evangelization and the three aspects outlined in the <u>Go and Make Disciples</u> document. If the project does not fit into one of the three categories, it should not be undertaken. But there is wiggle room in there as well. A pot luck supper, for example, while being a social function also works to build up the church community from within and is a family friendly and safe place to invite people to. As people learn to socialize and trust each other in relationships, they are more likely to volunteer and work together toward common goals on committees. The first tenet of the document talks about building up the community of the faithful through prayer groups, adult learning, etc. Socialization is part of being and building the parish community. But that isn't to say that the only activity within the church is social activity. There needs to be a balance of activities both spiritual and social. There also needs to be a balance of activities within all three arms of Evangelization – (1)- Building up the faith community; (2)- reaching out to those who are not in the community through the profession of the Gospel; (3)- doing acts of social justice so that you preach without using words. Unfortunately, many churches don't apply all three points

Limiting Factors

of Evangelization but focus in one area where they feel most comfortable and capable. For a church to grow, all three need to be addressed.

Getting back to the priest. Many of the older priests don't understand the term Evangelization. They may even think it is another program forced on them by some diocesan planning committee. Before you set your Evangelization proposal in action, before you present it to the priest, you need to have your ducks in a row. Do leg work, do research, check out what other parishes are doing. Have your goals in hand. Be able to present to him why you and your team think this is a good idea. Show him the benefits of what will happen and also tell him the costs involved so he can make an informed decision. Think things through carefully and don't sugar coat the outcomes, costs, time involvement etc. He is more likely to approve your notion IF you can present these things in a way that shows you are a leader and that you and the team are willing to make this commitment and not dump it back on him when you get tired of it. Be very honest, not only with yourselves about your expected outcomes and failings but with him. If you have a priest who is willing to let you try Evangelization tactics, consider yourself lucky indeed. You are ahead of the game.

Not all priests are open to Evangelization or lay leadership. Be persistent. Continue to engage him on how the Evangelization efforts will benefit the entire community. Start off small but persevere. Take your victories where you can, like when he allows you to put something in the bulletin, have an Evangelization fair or instructional session with the parish, or allows you to present in front of the congregation.

I made the mistake one time of being too persistent. Here's what not to do. I was coming up weekly with new ideas and presenting them to the priest. At one point, he saw me coming toward him after Mass and his eyes widened in fear. He picked up his cassocks and ran across the parking lot. "Yoo hoo Father! I have another idea" I said as I took off after him also at a dead run. Looking back, that was probably not the best approach to get things done. It probably was not one of my better, more graceful and grace-filled moments either although I'd get an "A+" for persistence. I have since learned from that episode and have tempered my approach to be slightly less pushy.

If the priest does not allow you to have an Evangelization committee or team, you can be part of existing ministries and share your thoughts through them and provide an "other centered" Evangelization outlook. Over time, the priest may relent. Being part of the other ministries allows them to see that you are not threatening their positions, authority or assigned job, but that you are there with an eye to the future. Don't get discouraged! I've said it before. Evangelization is like getting kicked in the teeth over and over again but bouncing back and coming at things from a different angle. Maybe all you can do in the beginning is a little thing like getting a small one-liner into the weekly bulletin.

Limiting Factors

It's a start. All things start small. You can build on the opportunities provided but don't give up! My close friend has been in a community where they are afraid of the word Evangelization because of all the TV evangelists that have given it a bad name. She feels like a whack-a-mole because her ideas keep getting shot down. Yet she still tries because there is a fire deep in her bones that needs to be heard so that the Gospel of Jesus can be proclaimed. She takes her victories where she can and assists in some of the social aspects of events while showing Evangelization through her service of others. Sometimes now, she even gets to propose an idea that gets accepted! But that didn't used to be the case. It's really tough trying to break through those preconceived notions and prejudices. Don't give up! Pray! Maybe God will use you as a catalyst for change.

At another juncture, I was part of an Adult Faith Formation Program. We were running programs the second Friday of each month based on what the parishioners had requested. We had quite a line-up of speakers and talks. The pastor of that parish told us not to have as many events, and that we needed to slow things down. We lost the momentum and fewer and fewer participants started showing up, because we were no longer consistently offering our programs. It went from the second Friday every month to once every three months and then petered out entirely. Even though he was on board in the beginning, he also was the one to pull the plug. I never really had a good reason why he felt as he did. It went from a successful, thriving program to dead in a very short time. Very sad.

Another limiting factor is the *team* you choose. Teams come about in many ways, probably as many as there are parishes. I have talked about team building in a previous chapter. Here I am just going to relay some of the limiting factors on a team that you would need to work around or adapt to in order to make things work. I know of an Evangelization team that doesn't drive at night except for one person. The events that they are able to do are limited to during the day or the weekends. In this case, the inability to drive at night is a limiting factor that needs to be considered before anything can be committed to.

Here is another example. There are people who go out with me as part of the street Evangelization who are sensitive to heat. I need to be careful to schedule these people to times when it is not the full heat of the day to protect them from a possible health issue. I also have several people on the team who are unable to walk very far. I need to make sure they have a chair to sit in and/or are positioned in an area where there will be traffic flow toward them.

If you only have yourself and one other person on the team, you are not very likely to be able to do big events. You will need to start out small and hope and **Pray** that more people will join you along the way. Your team is what you have to work with. Make the most of their talents and adapt to their limitations.

Limiting Factors

God has chosen you and them for this work. He can work through the limitations. You want to be able to plan things that you can reasonably accomplish. Yes, God provides others to assist, but you don't want to put yourself in a position where you are unable to meet your commitment either. It's like walking a fine line expecting the miracle of God's help but working on your own as if he won't give you one. If you have canvassed assistance through the bulletins, pulpit talks, Evangelization fairs, etc. and you have no one coming forward, you need to do what you and the limited resource of bodies are comfortably able to do. Don't plan an old-fashioned tent revival for thousands if you only have 2 people. This is why God gave us common sense too. Don't forget prayer. Prayer covers many inadequacies. How is God really leading you? Maybe he's telling you that the event you want can happen in the future but not yet. Maybe you need to learn to plan things on a smaller scale. Maybe you need to learn to trust the promptings of the Holy Spirit. There is any number of reasons why things may not go according to your plan. Don't throw away those ideas, keep them, but on the back burner, where you can pull them out at the right time. Trust that God sees the bigger picture and has the plan. You are given the opportunity to participate, but only at one step at a time. Remember Pope Francis said that part of Evangelization is proclaiming the message but in new and different ways. Keep the ideas coming and the prayers too. Learn from the events or things you do and grow forward.

Another limiting factor is *money*. Nobody wants to talk about money. Having a budget is really important. Let's face it. Everything costs money. Very little can be accomplished on a nothing budget except maybe putting one-liners into the bulletin or even having a full page printed up from the parish office. Anything you want to do will require some monetary investment. If you are fortunate to have a priest who is committed to Evangelization, he may give you funding as part of the church's vital functions. Most of you won't be that lucky. With lower church attendance in most areas, the collections are down and that means less money for overhead much less what the priest may perceive as other extraneous activities. He may be willing to give you a part of a particular collection or collections throughout the year. You could also do bake sales or movie nights with popcorn and treats to raise funds if the priest allows it. Be creative but work with the priest for what he would allow.

Another option to obtain funding is to pay for things yourselves. This is not the best option because then your program and ideas will not be acknowledged as adding value to the parish community and not acknowledged as an important ministry. The expectation will be that you will continue to pay for those things yourself. I say this also knowing that I myself have done just that. It shows that you are committed to the effort, "putting your money where your mouth is" so to speak. This needs to be prayerfully discerned also. It would still be best if you presented your ideas to the priest and

Limiting Factors

let him decide if the project or event is financially feasible and something that he is willing to support.

Another limiting factor is *time*. We all have a limited number of hours in the day. We have home and family responsibilities, jobs, children, care of elderly parents, etc. We all have things that tug at our time. It's part of being human and alive. But we also need to remember that we all are given the same number of hours in a day. How we choose to use those hours is up to us. Evangelization is not just a job, nor something to do in your free time, nor a way to rise up through the ranks in the church to be put into a position of authority. It is a way of life. Every aspect of your life is a point where you could be bringing the light of Jesus to others, by your words, your actions, even offering to pray for others. It's not just something that meets you in church on Sundays and then stays there when you leave. It is a joy of letting others know about Jesus. It is a need to proclaim the Gospel and share your story of how Jesus helped you in your life. It's a sharing of self, with all the vulnerability that comes with that, the sacrifice of self, to bring others into the shared experience of the Kingdom of God.

If you are starting an Evangelization effort, you already know the fire that is there to do "something" for God. There is so much to be done that you can't possibly do it all, not by yourself, not with a team of ten or twenty. God doesn't expect you to solve all the problems of the world. He just wants you to be ready and available to do His work to the best of your ability, even if it is small. Do things for the Kingdom with joy and love and He Himself will strengthen you. The last thing your church needs is for you to become burned out because of the aggressive Evangelization or ministry schedule you have set. It becomes important to do things with joy. If the joy goes away, or doesn't exist, you need to rethink what and how you are doing things. Even though we all want to save the world, we also need to take care of ourselves and our needs for rejuvenation. Some people find their peace in retreats, others in vacations or pilgrimages, others in daily walks. We are all different. Whatever makes you feel rejuvenated needs to be worked into your schedule so that you can be filled by God and experience the joy of Evangelization with renewed interest and gusto. A grumpy faced Catholic is not good for God's or the Church's public image and it could work itself into your heart to cause anger or bitterness. Also not good. Prioritizing what you do with your ministry time and down time are important. You can't do it all. Stepping back in a mental vacation is always a good way for new ideas to come forth too.

The Church has the same 24-hour day that the rest of us have. The Church cycles through the feasts and the ordinary times in the year. Summer barbeques and picnics, winter potluck suppers and movie nights. There is always something going on at Church, right? Things may slow down a bit in the summer time but try to schedule something and the calendar always seems to have some sort of conflict. So you've cleared up your schedule and

Limiting Factors

reassessed your priorities and know what you'd like to do and now you come across the guardian of the Church calendar – the church secretary. She holds onto dates with an iron fist. It reminds me of the scene from The Lord of the Rings when Gandalf says to the fire creature "You shall not pass." That is the secretary. She guards the Church calendar and also the priest's calendar with covetous jealousy. She tells you, "I'll get back to you," or "I'll make sure Father gets the message." You wait and you wait and try to be patient but you get no answer. Your request has fallen into the atmosphere and is gone. It leaves you wondering whether Father got the message and is busy or maybe he didn't get it. You try to send email this time and no response. You think it's just you she does this to but no, you speak with others and they have the same results. In the back of your head you hear the words 'be persistent,' but how long is an acceptable time to politely wait before you try again? I haven't figured that one out yet and just don't have the sense to quit. In any event, trying to get a date for something that everyone on the team can commit to and that the church has open is like pulling teeth, a long drawn-out and painful process. It's enough to discourage a person and tire you out before you even begin. But don't be discouraged. It's time to dig in with your heels and try another tactic. You could try to recruit her for your team and that may make things easier. Recruit the secretary's friends, bribe her with vegetables from your garden, etc. Working with the secretary flexes that creative muscle in your head which is good for building Evangelization ideas. I'm being facetious, but all kinds of obstacles can and will crop up to prevent you from achieving your goals. I do a disclaimer that this may not be the case in your church in which case you should consider yourself fortunate. Or maybe these things just happen to me. Hmmm.

Another limiting factor is the *one-size-fits-all* mentality. Just because something works in one church, does not mean it will work elsewhere. You may attend a conference or an event at another church (yes Catholics can go to churches other than their home parish) and be all fired up to do something similar in your home parish. You present the idea to your team, the priest, pastoral council, the powers that be, whoever they may be, and the idea flops. Or you get the go-ahead and it still flops for the day of the event. "What went wrong?" you wonder. "How did this not work?" The simple answer is because your church's personality and culture differs from the church you attended. One church may be heavily involved in social justice, another may do social activities primarily with little consideration for spirituality, another may be highly spiritual but lacking in community. You need to know how your church functions, the "persona" of your parish, in order to pick the best programs for you. God knows where you are. He also knows what He wants to do where you are and the best possible means to get there. Don't forget to tap into Him through prayer. If you develop events geared toward your particular needs, they

Limiting Factors

are more likely to be successful. Another point is that the ideas should come from the parish so that they can be involved from an idea's inception and be more committed to it. You can create a survey of needs for the types of things that people would like to see. In this needs assessment, include anything off-the-wall that you may have brainstormed with your team. You have no idea where it will lead. When you get the results of the survey, make sure you let the parishioners know that the things you hope to implement are directly based on their input, and also keep everyone informed throughout the process so they know their voices and thoughts were heard. There are numerous books written on surveys, statistics and how to involve the parish, so I won't belabor the point.

Another way to survey the parish without a written form to fill in is to have people set up at the doors of the church or even have an Evangelization fair where you can have team members talk to people in an impromptu and less threatening way to get people's ideas. Through the conversations about the pets that people are taking care of while their children are away (idea: dog walking service, pet grooming activity for teen ministry) or the sewing projects people are working on (idea: someone to make costumes for a church play) or the cakes someone made (idea: cake auction as a fundraiser!), you may come up with ideas for future activities and also a good estimation of people's strengths and giftings that they may otherwise not be willing to acknowledge. If someone tells you they do crafts, note them down! Crafters have an attention to detail, are self-motivated and think outside the box and are generally creative thinkers. These people can be contacted with some specific need in the future. Be open to the Holy Spirit's promptings to see how he uses these specific conversations. You can learn a lot about your parish by engaging the people in a non-threatening manner. Build future projects based on these. One size fits all just doesn't. Building your events from scratch will take some extra time and energy on your part but they are also more likely to succeed. Be creative. There is no one right answer or best way.

The last limiting factor I will speak about is *other people's reactions* to Evangelization. You may be in a church where they are progressive and really want to expand the church's reach beyond the doors and beyond Sunday. I can pretty much guarantee that that is not the norm. Most people hear the word Evangelization and all they can think of is the Tele-evangelists with all their antics up on center stage in front of thousands. Mention the word Evangelization to anyone in casual conversation and watch their eyes roll into the back of their heads as they quickly try to change the subject or get away from you. No self-respecting Catholic wants to be associated with THEM, the moonies, the born again Christians, bible-thumpers, the in-your-face Baptists or Hari Krishna. All lumped into the proverbial "them." You will have resistance to your Evangelization efforts unless you can find a way to reach the parishioners in a non-threatening

Limiting Factors

and gentle manner. Give talks on what Evangelization is. Maybe the priest would even be willing to do a series of talks on what it is, or maybe you can get a section in the bulletin as a weekly piece to talk about Evangelization in its different forms and how we are all called to share God's Word and love with others. Let parishioners know that Evangelization is doing the little things for God out of love. It's showing the fruits of the Holy Spirit in our daily lives. It's putting a smile on the face when you would much rather be grumpy or pull the blankets over your head. It's about one-on-one lending a helping hand to someone in need, like picking someone up who is walking on the side of the road who is obviously struggling with their groceries just to get home. It is watching someone's house while they are on vacation. It is lending an ear to someone who just needs to have someone to talk to. It is about being firmly rooted in the loving grace of Jesus and letting Jesus work through you in any situations that the day may bring as you interact with others. Not all Evangelization has to do with being able to make theological disputations and dispel notions through apologetics or recitation of scripture. Most Evangelization occurs between people and their one-on-one interactions. People will see how we live and be drawn to us by our humble joy, and knowledge that we are loved by God and so are they. It's not the big words that will impress anyone or the fancy bible that is carried under the arm, but the simplicity of a life that radiates God's presence. Parishioners need to be shown that they are, most likely, already doing these things as part of who they are as people and as Catholic Christians. No special training is needed to smile or greet new people when they come to Mass, to make people feel welcome. As conversations come about that they are not comfortable with, then those people can be referred to someone else like the priest, or someone who is on the Rite of Christian Initiation for Adults (RCIA) team or the Faith Formation/Religious Ed Coordinator. There are any number of avenues that can be tapped into that already exist within the church. It would also be appropriate for the parishioner to journey with this new person, depending on their relationship. Above all else, no one is alone. The backing of the particular parish community and 2000 years of Church are behind you. No one is expected to save the world. That's God's job. We, and all parishioners, only need to understand that small things count and that we all need to be willing to be used in each moment of each day. Are you the best self you can be in each moment? Are you open to God's leading? Do you love God enough to trust Him in all your dealings? That is Evangelization! Just let it flow out of you as part of who you are in your relationship with God. And that is what parishioners need to be made aware of. All else will fall into place as long as they are open to God's action in their lives and the life of the Church and your particular parish community.

Also ask the parishioners to pray for you as you venture forth in whatever you choose to do. Things that can't be accomplished through your own ef-

Limiting Factors

forts or force of will or intention can be done when God opens the door to you through prayer. Praying for others, while being part of the spiritual works of mercy, is also a large facet of what it means to evangelize. God magnifies those prayers and blesses your efforts.

As with the Evangelization team, there are poisonous people in the parishes. These are usually the ones who also complain the loudest. While you don't want to exclude them, you also don't want to focus a lot of attention to their particular complaints. Usually, those who complain are also the least likely to participate in anything, but fortunately, that percentage of people is very small. Hold fast and steady and continue your efforts while continuously explaining publicly what you are doing every step of the way. Remember, miracles do happen, even in the hardest of hearts.

One last point that I'd like to address in this chapter is Satan's tactics. Even though not a limiting factor in the strictest sense, he does try to limit your enthusiasm, accomplishments, progress, etc. just because he doesn't want you to succeed. The Hebrew word Shatan, from which our word Satan derives, means one who opposes God's will. If you are set on a course of Evangelization - bringing people into God's kingdom through the proclamation of the Gospel, you will instantly be under attack. It is nothing to be afraid of. We know that Jesus has overcome the world and Satan. No physical harm will come to you but you will be distracted in every way possible. For example, when we had our pep talk meeting to go over the materials our team would use when they went out on the street doing street Evangelization, one team member couldn't come because her dog stepped on glass and had to rushed to the vet. Another ended up with a sick child that needed to be rushed to the hospital because of an allergic reaction to a food substance. Another team member ended up with a dead car. Another one had the most horrendous day at work. You get the point. Everyone on the team had something happen immediately prior to the meeting. Satan uses all kinds of tactics to distract us from the work of Evangelization because he knows how our efforts will turn others toward God and that's the last thing he wants. He wants to keep control over people so that their focus is away from God and on themselves. This is why prayer is so important. We all learned a valuable lesson in prayer that day. You need to call God's mighty power down upon yourselves individually and collectively so that the fiery darts of the evil one don't hit you or anyone else. You need God's blessing and His protection as well. Satan also tries to cause arguments and division within the team because if you are fighting with each other, you won't be effective. You can't do it alone no matter how hard you try. My evening prayer every night covers my team in God's healing and protection so that we are bound by love and not divided by jealousies or other things that may come up. Satan also tries to tell you that everything will collapse without you, or he plays on any weakness that exists within you. This all is God's work.

Limiting Factors

Let Him orchestrate things. Just be ready to move when He does! But also recognize the way Satan tries to trick you.

Also, I need to say that if you are doing something that comes from your own head and it is not part of God's plan, good luck trying to get it done. Once God closes a door, you won't be able to open it, so don't even try. As things happen, as you plan events, be mindful of the obstacles that come along. Are they really big and insurmountable? Or are they minor inconveniences that you can get past or work-around? Insurmountable obstacles are a good sign that God is not in favor of your endeavor. Small ones may be Satan's tactics to keep you from doing God's good work. It's important to know the difference. Don't keep beating your head against a wall for no gain. Stop and pray. How is God talking to you through this situation? Does He want you to proceed? Did you lose your focus? Have you invited Him to be part of the process? Does He want you to shift priorities or stop altogether? Keep close to God and He will be close to you.

It's not always easy to do the work of Evangelization or to work with others. It is important to recognize that there will be obstacles, even with the best-intentioned. Nothing is impossible for God. Persevere and keep marching forward. Don't give up.

8

Street Evangelization

So after all this other talk about Evangelization teams and processes in the previous chapters, now I will begin to speak on street Evangelization. How the heck did I get here? I have no idea myself. I'm just tagging along for the ride. I certainly didn't want to start any new big projects. I had just had a brutal failure at starting a youth ministry program for the older teens and I was still licking my wounds. My team, God bless them all, kept saying to me "let's do this," "we can do this," "let's not be just pew potatoes because you can't evangelize anyone by sitting in the pews." Well, I had to agree with that last statement. You can't evangelize anyone new if you just see the four walls of the church. My first thought was to run away as far and as fast as I could. I remembered the story of Jonah where he didn't want to go to do what God said, ran in the opposite direction, got swallowed by a whale and deposited right where he was supposed to be in the first place. I figured that it would be just my luck to have a giant whale come get me where I am in this land-locked area of the state. Then I would have some serious explaining to do for sure. So I decided to go with the flow and jumped in with both feet, no whales in sight thankfully.

Donna Phipps

Our team toyed with the idea of making our own program. One of the team happened on the St. Paul Street Evangelization website. They are joy-filled Catholics going out onto the street to spread the Word of God. They had all kinds of materials already prepared, tracts on different subjects and a store where things could be purchased at deep discount prices. Plus, o joy of joys, they also provided all teams with a website where we could post blogs and keep the conversations going. Well, I was hooked at that point (pun intended). I had run out of excuses and now my natural curiosity was tentatively willing to move forward because I could see the potential and this was just the type of long term growing-the-church project I was looking for. I was still licking my wounds, that is why I was so tentative and tried to talk them out of it. I asked the team again if they were sure this is what they wanted to do. They assured me it was and they were gung-ho for doing this. I breathed a deep sigh and took the plunge. I made the contacts, took the tests, set up the website with all my personal adjustments to make it welcoming and inviting, ordered supplies and then waited for the longest winter on record to let go of its hold on the area so we could be outside. I didn't think the winter was ever going to let up. Everyone was chomping at the bit to get out and talk to people. It was all I could do to hold them back.

Then the day came. We took our table set up, our signs, our tracts and giveaways and went to a bus stop in the inner city where there was a lot of foot traffic. We finally got to talk to people! It was about

Street Evangelization

62 degrees outside. We learned a valuable lesson that day. Just because it's comfortable temperature, doesn't mean that the conditions are ideal. The wind was blowing at about 12 miles per hour. Our signs kept getting knocked over, tracts were flying. We had the brilliant idea to attach our signs to the tablecloth we had. Then things really got interesting. Our table looked like the flying nun as the wind caught the signs and started to lift everything. We looked more like the keystone cops than professional and serious evangelists. Remember how I said in an earlier chapter how nothing goes according to plan? This was definitely one of those times. I hope people watching us got a good laugh, anyway, if nothing else. I'm sure the main group at St. Paul's didn't have us in mind when they started this. They certainly didn't expect anything like our group. They might even revoke my privileges if they get wind of all of this. Through it all, we did manage to hand out a few prayer cards and tracts, and talked to a few people about the wonder and beauty of the Catholic Church. Only one woman yelled at us and told us to get away from her. Others politely said no or took a prayer card.

We also have what we call a secret weapon. We wear felt flames on our heads attached with wire. Yes, you are reading that right. Here is a picture of us wearing the flames. You can also see this picture in color on the back cover. The flames play on people's natural curiosity and invite them in to talk to us without our having to be in anyone's face. Once they come over and ask, we are able to engage them, offer a free prayer card and talk about what they want to talk about regarding the Catholic Church. The flames bring about some of the best conversations, I have found. Not everyone on the team will wear them but those of us that do have no problem being that fool for Christ that the apostle Paul called us to be. That should be obvious from some of the other stories I have relayed in this book.

Street Evangelization team first day outing.

Street Evangelization

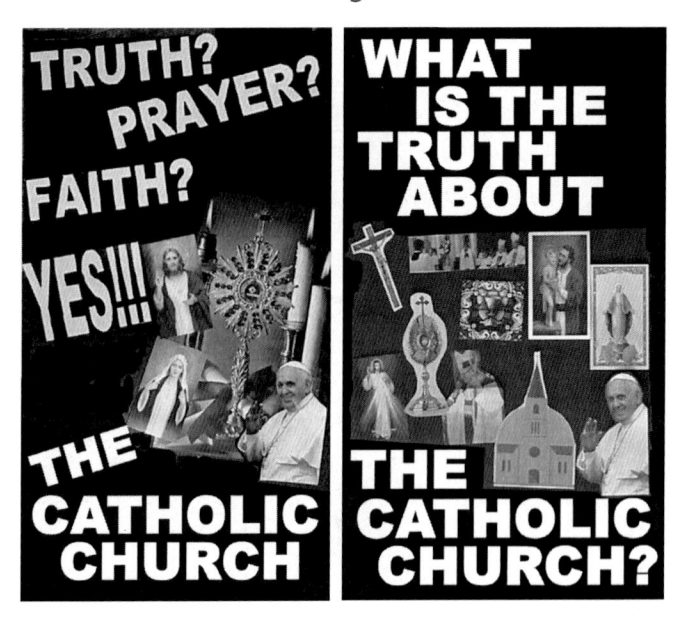

Here are pictures of the signs we made to go out.

And there was evening, the first day.

Two days later, we decided to go out again but to a different bus stop. We monitored the weather and saw that the wind speed levels were fairly low, less than 10 miles per hour anyway. We set up our table with the tracts and the other giveaways we had. There was foot traffic here. There was a strip mall and McDonalds close to the bus stop. We found the same thing as at the previous bus stop where people were politely refusing or accepting prayer cards. Some conversations took place where we invited people to come back to the Catholic Church for those who admitted they were Catholic but hadn't been in a while. We had a list of all the churches in the area so were able to direct people to a Catholic church closest to where they lived. Because of all the car traffic on the street and the way the noise seemed to resonate off the surrounding buildings, it was really difficult to hear the person we were trying to reach. For this reason and for no other, we determined that we would probably not come back to this particular spot.

We had a few interesting things happen while we were here. One woman saw the flames on our heads and commented that she couldn't believe the Catholic church had sunk so low that we had to wear flames on our heads. She said that she was a Catholic and couldn't believe what we were doing. My thought, and maybe I was wrong for thinking so, was that if she was a Catholic, she sure hasn't darkened the door of any church for many years. She wouldn't even take a prayer card from us. Very sad that she had so much animosity toward us. If she would have been the norm of the manner of person we encountered, it would be very discouraging. Thankfully, though, her attitude is not the norm. We had people cutting across four lanes of traffic just to ask us for rosaries and prayer cards as if they were going through the McDonald's drive-through. This happened about 6 times while we were out there. What was interesting also is that no one behind them beeped their horns in typical city, hurried, me-first fashion. The prayers we said before we started really seemed to be covering all of our efforts! One man, who had a very heavy accent and was apparently fairly new to this

Street Evangelization

country, received the prayer card from us and was reaching for his wallet. We told him it was free. He hugged the prayer card to his chest as if we had just handed him a great treasure. I realized at that moment how we take all the things we have in this country for granted. We are giving these things away for free that other people may not ever be able to see or receive. He gave me a far greater treasure by bringing the blessing of being in this great country to my thoughts.

We heard some really sad and terrible stories from people. We prayed over people when they asked for prayers and even referred someone to a local priest, whom I knew well, who would be able to pastorally assist their terrible situation.

Our time was about 2 hours.

And there was evening, the second day.

Our enthusiasm hasn't waned yet and we picked another bus stop to go to four days later. Also in the inner city with bus and foot traffic. We had our table set up and began walking among those waiting for the bus or getting off. It was very hot. We were trying to use the frame of the bus stop for shade. We had some interesting conversations, some people who were Protestant but were very tender-hearted toward us. I remember one nice girl who said she didn't want a prayer card. She then came back to us a few minutes later and apologized for being rude but that she was Christian and had a strong faith. She wanted us to know that she appreciated our efforts and wanted to be sure that we had cards to give out to others who may not have any faith.

Another store owner came running out to us with water. She said she was Catholic and new to the area so didn't know where to go to church. We told her where there was a church by her home. We gave her a rosary which she thanked us over and over for and told us what a blessing that was to her and what a blessing we were just by being there. She even said that if we came back to this area, that we could set up in front of her store where she would lower the awning for us so we would have shade.

There was much camaraderie in this area. This was a very ethnically mixed area. Even though this was just a bus stop, it appeared to be a community. They seemed to be really accepting of us being there with them. Some people couldn't read the prayer card so I read it to them and they studied the picture. Others asked whether it was ok to read the prayer since they weren't any good at memorizing. I said yes because God loves them and reads their hearts and knows how they feel.

We resolved to come back to this bus stop at some point because of the community we found there. Since we were just starting out, we wanted to explore our options further.

And there was evening, the third day.

The weekend was coming up but we had no specific plans. One of the team called me up and said

Street Evangelization

there is a Tulip Festival going on Saturday, and that maybe we could go there. Something inside me went off like fireworks and I said yes absolutely let's do this event where we can reach more people. After all, we had gone out three times already and had experience behind us now and we could handle this big event, right? This event was expected to draw 600,000 people. All those people to evangelize! I called the park authority and received permission to walk around although we didn't have permission to do a table. I converted our signs to ones we could now wear as placards around our necks. We had two teams for this event. Each team was going to do two hours, one team relieving the other. Carol, my husband and I were first. The second team also had three people. For last minute planning, I thought I had this one pretty well organized. How wrong I was! What a day!

My husband had dropped us off on the main street and said he was going to find parking. "Don't worry, I'll find you, just go set up" he said. We took all the signs, and tracts and prayer cards, bibles, extra giveaways, rosaries, etc., about 20 pounds worth and jumped out of the car. We walked into the park and prayed together. My courage was definitely failing me at this point. We donned our porto-signs and began to trudge along in the heat. We didn't get very far. Walking around carrying all this stuff was way too much. The heat and the humidity made it difficult to breathe. We got about 20 feet into the park from where my husband had dropped us off and we set up shop. It was a good spot, in the shade and lots of foot traffic streaming toward us. We offered and handed out prayer cards to everyone that passed. One of the first people we spoke with had been a Catholic but had left the church. He had asked us whether the Church still did stations of the cross. I said yes. As he was walking away, I realized I had a give-away copy of the stations of the cross, part of that 20-pound lead weight in my bag, because we were prepared for anything and had all manner of things stuffed into our grand valise of Catholicism. We were prepared for anything because we didn't know what conversations people will throw at us. So Carol, who is 77, took off after him at a good trot but lost him in the crowd. Dang it! We had missed that opportunity! Was this the way the day was going to go? Time was about 1:15 in the afternoon. We had scheduled our time there from 1-5pm.

   I'm going to back up a little here. The team had agreed that we would communicate for the day using cell phones. I'm not very cell phone savvy, let's start there. I figured it rings, you answer it, so how hard can that be? I made sure we all had each other's numbers. I had never been to this park and said I would call them when I had a spot so they could find me. I figured "how big could this park be?" There is a land mark in the park, a statue of Moses. Where we set up was in the first line of trees straight back from his back. I called everyone and told them where I was. Then Carol and I settled in to do some serious evangelizing.

Street Evangelization

About an hour into it, we realized my husband still hadn't found us. I saw him at one point in the distance but he never came our way. That was the last I saw him until much later in the evening. I was also starting to wonder at this point why I had thought this festival was a good idea.

Three o'clock came and went when our relief was supposed to arrive. I called them, I think. My brain cells were starting to only fire sporadically at this point. They said they were looking for parking and would be there shortly. The other member of that team had left me a voice mail saying she was in the park. I had never heard the phone ring and thought it was because the music was so loud. I called her back, she didn't answer. I knew they were all on the way. Hooray!

By about 4pm, everything was shutting down. Backs, legs and smiles all gave out. Carol and I gave up. We turned the signs around and just sat in the grass. Done. Finished. Hot. Getting grumpy, certainly not the face of a good evangelist. Around 4:30 half of the second team arrived. I found it odd that my husband was nowhere in sight. I called him at home and there he was! He had abandoned me! In his defense he knew that the only way to reach him would be if he were home since only I had the cell phone. There were other people who were going to join us in the park as well and he said they were there looking for me but couldn't find me. Trees. Moses. I thought I had made it clear. Sigh. My husband showed back up at 5:30 to pick us up at a better prearranged spot this time – the donut shop on the corner.

We had some interesting conversations throughout the day. Two young ladies stopped to talk to us and said that they were Jewish and had no understanding of Christianity. One of the second team was a convert from Judaism and was able to engage them in good conversation. We had people who would not take prayer cards from us until they found out we were Catholic but were afraid to ask if we were. I offered one person a prayer card, who, I'm positive was a Satanist. He took the card and put it in his pocket. I thought "o boy, that probably was not a good idea." I then remembered the story I had heard at a conference of one woman who was a Satanist and someone stepped out in faith 20 years ago and gave her a brief introduction to Jesus. It took 15 years for those words to sink in but when they did, she became an Episcopalian and then finally a Catholic. So even though in my head I was going "O God, O God, O God what have I done?!?!?!?" I was reminded and comforted by remembering that woman's story that it took 15 years for her seed to materialize. Maybe something similar would happen with him. All we need to do is plant the seed and let God do the rest.

We had just spent the day handing out cards, about 300 of them. I realized that everyone we handed a card to was a missed opportunity to contact us through our website because our contact information was not on the cards. DOH! Then I also figured out why I never heard the phone ring. It was on vibrate and sitting in the bag on the ground. DOH!

Street Evangelization

Evening came (thankfully and finally), the fourth day.

Undaunted by our recent escapade, we made another attempt at a big event, though not quite as big as the Tulip Festival. We went to the Canal Fest held on the following weekend. I was watching the weather like a hawk. It was raining and miserable all week so we hadn't had an outing and were chomping at the bit. The morning of the festival was going to be raining. Lo and behold, the hours we were going to do seemed to clear up, as if God was opening up a window of opportunity for us. Or maybe He just needed another laugh, I'm not sure which. I had also made another sign to set up in front of the table that had our website information on it for anyone who may not stop to talk to us but would see our contact information, be curious and look us up. I was hoping anyway. Just one more level of being prepared.

We agreed to try doing the two teams again with one relieving the other. My husband and I did first shift and Carol and Helen were on second. We got there and set up our table on the outskirts of the festival because I had not been able to reach anyone in the city government to get approval. I knew we were allowed on public streets and parks. We were about 2 feet away from a public street in the spot we picked to set up. I was hoping no one official would notice.

My husband stood at the table with the tracts and I stood in the stream of the people flow. I had

This sign was made as a sandwich board to stand up on its own and had the same information on both sides.

some interesting conversations and handed out about 100 prayer cards. Carol and Helen found us no problem, thank God, and we made the switch. Hooray it worked!

When the event was over, Helen dropped all the equipment off at my house and then told me that a park official seemed like he was eyeballing our little display with bad intent as if he were going to turn us in for violating park code or something. I had my cell phone with me and remembered to turn it on this time, in the event there was an issue. But, perhaps he thought better of it and let it go. Or maybe God stretched out a helping hand on our behalf. I don't know but am thankful it didn't get ugly. We ended up handing out 250 prayer cards for the day. This time, they all had our web contact information handwritten on them.

Evening came, the fifth day.

The Spirit is still strong with us and our enthusiasm is not waning. We presented what the team is doing to the local deanery of priests. They seemed generally enthusiastic about what we were trying to accomplish, especially since we weren't asking them to do anything or back us financially. With that behind us now, we were gearing up for the local Memorial Day Parade. I set up shop on the steps of my home parish. Very quickly we realized that there would only be a few people within our immediate vicinity. Carol and Helen took off at a good trot in opposite directions, handing out fish and prayer cards. The fish and the prayer cards now had our contact information on them and the fish had a scripture passage on them as well. To date, we only handed out about 5 fish. We decided after the Tulip Festival to call the fish "bookmarks" to increase their appeal.

Carol walked up one side and down the other. She came back with a huge grin on her face saying, "I like parades, because they are a captive audience."

She had a point. People were settled down into their spots and starting conversations was easy. We handed out rosaries, prayer cards and fish. The parade wasn't bad either.

Evening came, the sixth day. And so it began...

9

Musings and Lessons Learned

This has been a crazy road and a wild adventure doing the work of Evangelization. As I write this, my house is in chaos because of the varying stages of fish production strewn throughout as we try to churn through them by the thousands to meet our needs. Every table-like surface is taken up by fish parts, prayer cards and Evangelization supplies. I have whole bags of rosaries with the instructions. I have boxes of prayer cards ready to go too. I have more bags of Marian and St. Anthony jewelry and prayer cards that each one of us gets from the various missions and Catholic associations because once you give to one, they all get your name on a list and they keep sending you these freebies. So all of those are ready to go on the street. Then in another stack I have the local Catholic paper that I haven't had a chance to read since February. That pile keeps growing too. Thank God my husband is a patient man and has eyes only for me and not these endless piles that are all over. It's really embarrassing having anyone other than the team visit because they wonder what is wrong with me and why the house is in the state it is. My consolation is that everyone on the team also has fish parts all over their houses too. Right now, when we do an event, we are handing out about 200-300 prayer cards and about 50-100 fish.

Sample of a fish.

I remember how the fish came about. Carol and I set up a table at the yearly diocesan training event. The theme was "Fishers of men." We were on the diocesan Evangelization committee at the time and set up this table to talk to people about Evangelization. We wracked our brains trying to come up with things that we could do on the cheap. We decided to set up a display as if we were fishing. You can see the picture that follows of our set up. We set up nets and fishing poles and cut out spongy fish and attached them to the nets. Then she says to me. "I have an off-the-wall idea." I always love her off-the-wall ideas, because it is always something interesting, that will make people think and invariably throw me into the soup, or into the fire storm that follows. It's a lot more interesting than sitting on the sidelines, I sure can tell you. I was already "hooked." She said "why don't we make fish to hand out to people as a giveaway? They could have a scripture quote from Jesus' words in the Gospels (you know, the ones written in red) on one side and our team contact information on the other." Sounded good to me. We went out and bought 14 sheets of poster board from the local Dollar store at $.50 each. We bought neon red craft string on clearance because the neon red was symbolic of the Holy Spirit and huge bags of beads also on clearance. We started to trace and cut and glue fish. We added 3 beads each, symbolic of the Holy Trinity. That's where it all began. Carol kept joking with me saying that we were going to take the fish on the road someday because they'd be so popular. That was a period of practice, because now we are in the big leagues of production. We ended up with about 700 fish to give away during this first event which cost about $.07 each. After the fish were assembled, we took one as a sample of the whole to be prayed over by two different charismatic groups in the area. We asked them to pray over the fish and also us as a team.

After the event was over and we still had 500 or so fish, I stuck them in my basement. I pulled out a few each year to hand out to my kids that I was teaching in the first year confirmation class, redone with the symbols of the creed on them as a visual reminder of our class. That's a subject for another

Donna Phipps

Our "Fishers of Men" setup.

time. But there they sat in the basement. We were wondering why we had made so many.

After the initial event, the following year, the diocese had another event and the theme was the "Fire of the Holy Spirit." That is where we came up with the ideas of wearing flames on our heads. I had made 8 of them for us but people who came to the event wanted them so we handed them out. Who knew that my little cheap $.05 flame headpiece would be so popular? We also pulled out the fish for this event as well. We had one woman come up to us and ask us if she could reproduce the fish. She was part of a missionary group. We told her yes. I don't know whatever happened with that. After the event I put the flames aside as well and I would pull these out when I taught the section on the Holy Spirit to the Confirmation class.

If we knew then what God had planned for us now, we might have taken the chance and run like heck. We were only allowed to see a small portion of what we were to do. God lit one step in front of us and that is what we did. It is obvious, looking back now, that there was a bigger plan in place. There might be an even bigger one still that we can't begin to imagine. Here we are just taking one step forward and doing what He tells us in that step. If we saw the bigger picture, it would be frightening. Who would have thought that these silly little paper fish could become a rallying point for bringing His people back to Himself? Yet that's what seems to be happening. Four years after the first event, I also received a phone call from the local Catholic radio station asking me to send them 25 fish. She still had her fish from the event and was consoled each day by the words from scripture that were written there! Watching God's hand at work, and how He can use our inadequate efforts, our failings and weaknesses is truly humbling. And paper fish! Who would have thought that my life's work summed up is in making paper fish! It's a good thing I got an "A" in cut and paste in kindergarten then, isn't it?

I am reminded of the scene from the Wizard of Oz, when the witch releases her flying monkeys and says "Fly, fly my pretties." The same thing, and just as scary but for different reasons, seems to be taking place with the fish. They are being released into a people starving for the truth and with no consolation. They are God's mighty power at work through the simplicity of a paper fish.

I am also noticing that the days we choose to go out, when it is acceptable to God, even though it may be raining the rest of the day, the hours we decided on are clear. We call these windows of opportunity or times when God is smiling down on our efforts. Also, because of heat sensitivities, we need to watch the temperature. Higher humidity will drain our energy faster than just heat alone, which means that we can do about an hour instead of two.

Now that we are going on the street two or three times a week, we've used up all the stock we had and can barely keep up with the need for them as we go out. People seem to really like them because they are cute, clever and colorful. Another thing we are finding that continuously blows our minds is that people come back to us, sometimes in tears, sometimes laughing that the words on the fish were exactly what they needed at that time. This has happened over and over again. In fact, when I make them, I pray over them, many times saying "your words will not come back to you void." As I write this, we have about twenty-eight people doing the varying stages of fish production.

Another interesting thing I am finding is that people generally want to help. They may not feel capable of going out on the street, but they want to assist in the process somehow because they see value in what we are doing. I have people on the team who pray for us, others have severe physical handicaps who can maybe only cut the string or the address labels or tie on the string to the fish. As I said previously, these are the people God has chosen and called forth for me to work with in this ministry. It can be frustrating showing that one person over and over again how to cut and measure string. But at the same time there is a very humbling element in that because of her desire and willingness to do something for the Kingdom no matter how small. I also consider that this may be the only opportunity this person has to do something for God's Kingdom and that this could be the task for her where God says to her at her death, "well done good and faithful servant." I am reminded of the passage from scripture which says to him whom much is given, much is expected (Luke 12:48). Although it would be really easy for me to say I'm too busy to help her or someone else like her, the truth is, this work of Evangelization is all about making connections with others. As I am out on the street making new connections, I can't forget about the ones who are doing their best to help. Evangelization is about all of us working together and lifting each other up in the process. So I take the few minutes or so it takes to come up with a new way to teach her or to help her along, and I thank God that she is there to keep me humble. "There, but for the grace of God go I."

I am also noticing that the fish makers are forming a community with each other when before we were all strangers. If someone is sick, one of the other team members goes to visit. Of the twenty-eight or so people working on this, we are mostly, what the world considers, throw-away people with our various disabilities, malfunctions and frailties. We all are less than perfect by the world's standards. As people, we all need the encouragement that a community provides. And we all have something to offer, no matter how small and seemingly insignificant. We all do what we can do to the best of our abilities. So even though most people don't seem broken, we are those broken in body ministering to those broken in faith or spirit. As a side note, I believe we are also not seen as threatening and people are more willing to listen to us because our brokenness is so apparent when we go out on the street.

When we go out, we can effectively handle about two to two and a half hours. After that we get tired and grumpy, which doesn't make for good Evangelization. The good news is that we are not punching a clock with anyone but God. He knows our hearts and our efforts and also our limitations. He knows that we are trying to serve Him. It's not about racking up the hours or winning brownie points but doing the best we can in each immediate moment, and being available for His service by His grace.

Our team went out on the street fifteen times in a month and a half. Each time we go out is different. There are some really nasty people out there. Overall though, we are strengthened and empowered by those who are supportive of our efforts and receptive to the Word of God. Even when there are days of all nasty people like I had recently, the overall experience is very positive and uplifting, which makes me want to go out again and again. There is a tremendous sense of fulfillment, that I wouldn't have imagined possible by being in the trenches of sharing God's Word with others. If you would have asked me a few months ago, where I would find joy, my answer certainly would not have been by being on the street. Here I am. Eager for each opportunity. Greedily watching the weather each day for those windows of blessing when I can be back out among God's people.

Just when we think we have it figured out and we're assuredly and calmly moving along, God throws another curve ball at us. I found myself in a typical "you want me to do what?!?!?!" moment the other day while in prayer. God said we needed to increase production and make MANY more fish because 1000 fish strewn all over my house is not enough. I did all the centering prayer and cleansings I could think of. "Whatever is not from God... Jesus, Jesus, Jesus, Jesus not me but you," etc. You get the idea. There it was again. "You need to make MANY more fish." What does many mean? I know what I teach many to be. Jesus came for many because not everyone would accept Him. I didn't think that was the meaning I was after. Then I remembered the other meaning of "many" from biblical times of too many to be counted. O boy. What the heck does that mean for what's coming down the road??? As I write this, I have no idea what is in store or how soon. I do know that the heads-up doesn't give a lot of lead time or planning time usually. Something really BIG is coming. I'm seriously thinking of taking my chances with the whale this time.

10

Musings On People

When choosing where to go for our efforts, I understand the need for relationships and being consistent. But, to me, there is something thrilling about being in a big event with hundreds of thousands of people attending, all possibilities of sharing the salvific power of our Lord. The Tulip Festival has not dampened my enthusiasm for these events. I see these big events as windows of seed planting, like the heads of dandelions that get carried away in the wind. Yet I found, as did Carol, that there is a strange paradox at these events. You would think that while participating in recreational or leisure activities that people would be, well, leisurely. The same rush and bustle goes on at these events as occurs during New York City rush hour. Everyone is trying to get someplace in time for something. Very little real, interpersonal communication goes on. We give out 200-400 cards and materials yet may have only one or two conversations. Also interesting to me is that I tend to be a home body and these type of events hold no interest for me for my own leisure planned outings. Yet, when the Lord fires me up, I am the first one ready to go. Usually on very short notice too! That in itself is amazing to me. God takes even our brokenness and semi-willingness and uses it. It becomes very apparent that it is not by our own power that anything gets done but God Himself.

I really like going to the bus stops in the inner city. People are far more willing to talk to you. They seem to be a captive audience as they wait for the bus and are willing to share thoughts and listen. Sometimes they don't even care if they miss a bus, because there will be another one. Just like the parades, they are more calm. It is a different story with those getting off the bus. Very rarely can we engage those people in conversation.

We had a situation occur the other day at a bus stop. One person, kept me talking for almost 45 minutes. There were two of us at the stop. It was difficult to get away from him without being rude. When I was able to politely extricate myself, we beat a hasty retreat away from the location. I realized then that there could be situations like this one that would come up and that we as a team needed to work out some kind of code where we would know one of us needed help. We're still working on the specifics but one of the things that episode taught us is awareness of each other and a need to be close to each other. Not to say that the conversation was bad or that he was threatening but he was definitely getting a little overly chummy with me. I was reminded of another lesson I learned early on in this street ministry process. I was so enthusiastic of talking to another soul and potentially bringing them to Christ that I handed out my home phone number. That definitely was a mistake. This guy probably lost it which was a good thing but the lesson was learned. It could have potentially been a very bad situation. Now, we do not have our private emails and information on anything we give away. My husband set up our website and contact information to be a totally new account that can't be traced back to us. God wants us to be available but not to be stupid and so He gives us these lessons so that when similar situations occur, we are ready and that we are not needlessly putting ourselves in danger.

I always find it interesting that the people we talk to are the ones we individually are meant to. It amazes me how God orchestrates our lives so that the situations we experience can be used in connecting with people. Here are two examples of things that happened recently. I was talking with one man who was looking for a bagel shop. I could tell he was from New York City, as was I. I commiserated with him and said that I wasn't able to find any decent bagels since I moved away from there. He said that he was in search of a specialty shop which was a few stores down from where we were. I wasn't familiar with it but asked him to come back and tell me when he found it. We had a nice chat about why I was there on the street. He took a prayer card and went his way. He came back a few minutes later and told me he had found the shop and then wished me blessing. The other team member had an occasion to speak with a Quaker. She was familiar with the banquet hall the Quakers rented out to the public as a fund raiser. I never would have known that but she did and it made a connection with this person.

Other times we were in situations that only could have been orchestrated by God. We did an event which was a free summer concert series. I found myself getting progressively uncomfortable because of the free flowing alcohol that was going on. During this time, I saw the young woman who had been my student for RCIA (Rite of Christian Initiation for Adults) just a few months prior. She told me that her parents had tragically died in a motorcycle accident. I was glad I was able to be there for her and offer her prayer and some comfort. On that same day, Carol spoke with someone who was so thrilled to see Catholics on the street evangelizing. She said she was going to bring her mother the following week and took a rosary and prayer card for her. Carol agreed to pray for her. We found out later in the week that the mother died. I hope that she was comforted by the rosary and knowing that we were praying for her. Even though we don't have any intention of going back there, we were apparently right where we were needed at that time. Most times the results of our efforts are not so obvious but this was a moment of consolation that we were in the right place at the right time.

Some other thoughts on people that I have found interesting and that I'd like to pass on. We have been out on the street and said hello to people who passed. They ignored us the first time or pretended to be too macho or cool to pay attention. As

Musings On People

we stood there, even within the same day, as they passed by again a second or a third time, they were more likely to open up and say hello. It was that familiarity of just standing there that made them comfortable. This happened at the Tulip Festival where the third time someone passed us, he came and asked for a card when he wouldn't even say anything the first time he passed.

We also hear some interesting excuses from people who can't stop to talk to us or take a prayer card. "My hands are full," is a good one, "No, I'm good" is common, but the best one is "I already have one at home." Not likely since the prayers we hand out are as unique as the fish. But we understand that talking about religion could be difficult for some people and we accept those as a polite no and leave it at that.

One example of people's general goodness. We had a new woman start on the team. She was really nervous about handing out prayer cards. I shadowed her to put her at ease. We were at a bus stop handing out the cards. I told the people there that it was her first time out. They were all strangers to me and possibly not even Catholic, yet they applauded her and told her she was doing a great job. These are the times that make all our efforts worthwhile.

One sad point I have about doing the street ministry the way we are is that we don't have any way of following up with people to see if they went to Mass, or talked to whichever priest we may have referred them to, or even got an answer to their prayers as we pray for them. Maybe we will reconnect somewhere with these people, but, for now, they are chance encounters mostly. God's chance which means there are no coincidences but limited encounters just the same.

11

Social Justice

The Catholic Church does social justice really well. It's as if it becomes embedded in our very marrow. If you see someone in need or in trouble your reaction is to offer your assistance. Catholics, as a whole, tend to be more generous with their time and their money in helping the poor and those who are less fortunate. It could well be said that the impetus to do social justice came from Jesus when He told us to do unto others as we would have them do unto us, and whatever you do to the least of these, you do for me. In this chapter, I would like to explore some of the ways your church can take on a Social Justice activity. Incidentally, when Acquired Immune Deficiency Syndrome (AIDS) first became widespread, it was the Catholics who set out to serve their needs and took the risks of infection even before the vectors were completely understood. I was working with an AIDS researcher at the time and this was one of the interesting points that we came across.

One of the most common things for a church community to do, especially in the urban areas, is to have a food pantry. This is a relatively easy project and promotes good will for the Catholic Church in the local area. Even though this is the most common form of social outreach, there are hundreds of things that could be done if you have the time, money, manpower, imagination, etc. to make it happen. I just recently discovered a volunteer network on the online networking site LinkedIn. My husband is a member and recently was solicited for assistance as a volunteer for literacy. There are hundreds of volunteer opportunities offered through this site. This may be a good starting point to generate ideas for your parish activity. Another good source of material for social justice activities comes from the corporal and spiritual works of mercy and the beatitudes. I will go through some of these and list ideas for things that can be done in each area.

The Beatitudes

Blessed are the poor in spirit, for theirs is the kingdom of heaven.

What does it mean to be poor in spirit? I know that theologians wrestle with this question. In my mind, anyone poor in spirit could be someone who doesn't have full use of their faculties, maybe they feel beaten down by life and circumstances, are homeless or maybe they have mental illness, or even experienced abuses as children or adults. This opens up a whole area of exploration for things that your parish can do, both locally and globally. Locally, you could assist at battered women's shelters. You could collect clothing and personal items for said shelter. Another aspect would be to provide speakers in self-help and confidence building, provide help with basic life skills like budgeting, finding and holding a job, resume writing, "dressing for success," and legal assistance if anyone in the community has legal training. For children who are impoverished or abused, you could work with authorities to help with some of their programs. Another way to work with children is in the terminal pediatrics ward at your local hospital. These children don't get to play like healthy children and are stuck in an environment of needles and pokings all the time. You may want to volunteer your time for one-on-one time with them, put on puppet shows, bring some activities in like clowns or jugglers to help them deal with the stresses of being sick. If your church has a school attached, you may also have one or more of your classes "adopt" the ward and send get well cards. Many of these same ideas could also be translated well to a mental health unit, or even a long term care facility for the elderly or those with birth defects or even war veterans. I would caution you, though, against involving children with the mentally ill because of the diversity of the diseases involved and the unpredictability of behaviors, perhaps this would be best as an adult-only activity. Globally, *Cross Catholic Outreach* and *Food For the Poor* are two programs that I know of which collect food for the hungry in other countries, but there are hundreds of such programs. Some of these missionary efforts offer an "adopt a child" or some such program where you can become sister parishes with a foreign church so that everything you collect goes right to them. There are countries in the world which still practice slavery. Efforts could be made toward global equality, women's rights, etc. I recently discovered a prayer to St. Josephine Bakhita who was enslaved. These prayer cards could be distributed in bulk to the oppressed who could benefit from her intercession.

I know of one woman who brings sandwiches to those who are living on the street. I know of other people who open their doors and take in some of the homeless and help them get on their feet. I myself have picked up women hitchhikers, obviously struggling to get their groceries home. The doors are wide open here. You may choose to start a hospital program for sick children and collect things like blankets, books or stuffed animals. The bottom line is that the best program is the one that is sustainable by your church and that you feel the Holy Spirit is leading you to.

Blessed are the meek for they shall inherit the land.

Ok so I have inherited the land but what am I supposed to do with it? I don't know that I have anything to say about the meek but I will talk briefly about land here. In this section you could teach people how to cook vegetables, help set up community gardens where people learn to grow their own food. Land could also mean taking care of possessions like offering cheap car repair for those who are struggling, setting up a program to con-

Social Justice

nect people with car donations to help them get to work. Maybe it means giving cooking classes to help people who are making do with less. Maybe it's talking to people about making good food choices, or cooking meals for families where they can have a more wholesome option other than fast food for dinner, but cheap enough where it won't break the bank.

I knew of a church who used to get a fairly large group of people together. They then went to an underprivileged area and would rake leaves, and do general clean-up work in the area. They wouldn't be deliberately speaking about scripture or Jesus, but inevitably, people in the area would question them and then the conversations would begin of why they were doing what they were doing, which was to show the love of Jesus. By their actions they were known as true Christians and drew people in who otherwise would not have had that exposure.

Blessed are they who hunger and thirst for righteousness, for they will be satisfied.

Righteousness. There are so many evils in this world. Where do you begin? Anti- abortion activities would be the first that comes to my mind both locally and nationally when marches are organized in Washington D.C. If you have any political inclinations, you could work with local politicians to improve housing, jobs, laws, fracking practices, etc. There is no limit to the things that could be addressed or that you could put your hands to. Our governments, both local and Federal, have many areas where human dignity concerns need to be brought to the light. Other areas for political interaction and edification on human dignity would be the death penalty, immigration and minimum wage. The need is almost endless.

Blessed are the clean of heart for they will see God.

When you are struggling with addictions or other things that keep you focused on yourself, it is difficult to focus on God and have a clean heart. People struggle with all kinds of things. Some people feel they are so bad off that God couldn't possibly want anything to do with them. Addictions come in all forms. Alcohol, drugs, gambling, food, sex to list a few. People need to hear the truth that God loves them. They also need to know that they're not alone in their struggles and that someone really cares for them. This is a hard ministry road to follow with many pitfalls and disappointments because you are not going to be able to do all things for all people. You may have moments of breakthrough but many more disappointments. If you feel strongly that God is calling you to this, don't give up and remember that you yourself are not alone but have a vast array of social systems and professionals to support your efforts as you help to support those struggling with addictions. One way to help may be to volunteer in a withdrawal clinic, or the local halfway house once people are released from the main program. Perhaps you could get a group of people together who would be willing to make a

Social Justice

meal for those housed there once per week or once per month as time permits.

Blessed are the peacemakers, for they will be called children of God.

I can see doing ecumenical and interfaith rallies for peace as part of this. I can also see developing ties with non-Christian religious groups for the purpose of peaceful cooperation. I can even see aiding in racially charged situations to provide solidarity and unity and community. Even providing sandwiches to peaceful demonstrations would be a way to breach the distances between people.

Blessed are they who are persecuted for the sake of righteousness, for theirs is the kingdom of heaven.

I'm not really much into persecution, but I do know that there are people who are wrongfully accused of crimes. Advocacy programs and support systems could be developed to help the victims and families in such situations.

Blessed are the merciful for they will be shown mercy.

Blessed are they who mourn for they will be comforted.

I will include the corporal and spiritual works of mercy in this category. There are innumerable possibilities here.

Donna Phipps

Corporal Works of Mercy

Feeding the hungry - food pantries, soup kitchens, bringing meals to those who have surgery and can't cook for themselves, gift cards to the local grocery store. Globally, things like rice bowl or UNICEF.

Giving drink to the thirsty - passing out water bottles to local migrant workers or construction workers, or anyone else who may work outside during the heat of the day. Globally, working toward clean water sources.

Sheltering the homeless - We have already covered this in part under the first beatitude. One thought could be a blanket drive with a coupon for a free meal attached to the blanket as part of the drive. Habitat for Humanity is one example of a good program that is doing this. There may be other organizations that may be local to your area as well. I also know of an ecumenical Youth Ministry effort where they go to low income areas and perform repairs and renovations to homes in an effort to assist needy and low income families.

Clothing the naked - I lived in an area awhile back where the local church would give away free clothes to everyone who needed them every Tuesday morning. All they needed to do this was an appropriate space and a few volunteers.

Here is an inspiring story that didn't cost anything to the coordinator except time and innovation. I will call the person "Mary." Mary and a woman she worked with at a local convenience store decided to do a Christmas party and make mittens for the low income kids in the local pre-kindergarten and Head Start programs as a welcome to the new neighbor initiative. They thought it was only a few kids and it turned out to be 150 in the daycare and 200 in the Head Start program. This was obviously more than they expected or more than they could do by themselves. For whatever reason, the partner in this endeavor backed out so it left Mary to do this effort by herself. Not daunted by this task, she called the local nursing home and the Department of the Aging to request women who were still able to knit or crochet mittens for the children. Both groups agreed. Now she needed to acquire all the yarn that would be necessary to complete the project. She went to the local elementary school and all the children were asked to bring in yarn leftovers from their mothers' projects. Yarn was donated by the bagful! The Junior High School got wind of this project and volunteered to make cookies for the children's Christmas party. Mary approached her employer in several store locations and received donations of flour, sugar, butter and the rest of the ingredients needed to make cookies and serve juice as refreshments during the Christmas party. At this time the Senior High School class also wanted to get involved and agreed to sing for the children as part of their chorus. In addition, Mary asked the local seniors whom she knew had a clown unit, to perform for the party. Everything came together and the children had awe and appreciation on their faces and laughter for the day. This project went on for several years and kept growing until several counties were involved. Mary even roped her son into dressing up as a bear to perform for the children doing counter steps to what a dance group from the seniors was doing. The looks on the children's faces made all the effort worthwhile. The children, in turn, repaid the contributors in the nursing home by sending them thank you cards and making paper chains for their decoration. All this was possible because of one person's ingenuity and persistence.

Visiting the sick - This applies either in the Hospital or when they return to their homes. Alzheimer's is a sickness too and people with dementia and other age-related mental diseases respond well to visits and stimulation to keep their minds active. I remember playing cards with a woman who had Alzheimer's. She couldn't remember the rules but knew she loved to play. I, with great affection, called her the cheatingest old lady ever but I knew she couldn't help it and just liked to play. We would play for hours on end and the rules would change with each hand. But it made her so happy.

One of the local churches has a knitting group that makes shawls and hats for cancer patients and pray over them as they go. A note is attached to each shawl to let the recipient know that the item was prayed over in love.

Visiting the imprisoned - Prison ministry is an important part of outreach. Bringing a little God into people's lives even when they are judicially proclaimed sinners may be valuable to their personal development as people. Please make sure you check with the local prison authorities before you do anything in this area and work closely within the guidelines that are established for your, the prisoner's and the guards' safety.

Burying the dead - Within this facet, you could offer classes to help people start planning for end of life issues. It could include information on wills, living wills, funeral choices made before your death so your grieving family doesn't have to make the decision. You can also include the importance of life insurance, how and where to purchase a cemetery plot. You may also offer services to assist the family for planning for the burial Mass and what would be involved on the day of the funeral. You can have pre-printed booklets for the people to follow during the Mass since a good portion of those who attend funeral Masses are not Catholic. By having the booklet preprinted ahead of time, it would make the activities of the Mass easier to follow. You would just need to insert the particular readings they chose and include descriptions of the actions expected at each part. As the church's representative, you could also provide names of grief counselors in your area.

Spiritual Works of Mercy

Instructing the ignorant - Aren't we all ignorant in something? I chose to teach the ninth grade Confirmation class. I also teach Rite of Christian Initiation for Adults (RCIA) to help people understand the Church and grow in love and faith. Within this context, again, there are many possibilities of where you can apply your teaching skills or assist in people's personal development. You could help set up a reading program to teach adults how to read. You can work with officials to set up immigration programs to teach immigrants how to become citizens if you have a particular love of history. Maybe you can speak a foreign tongue and there are many immigrants within your area who speak that language that you could help them learn English. Programs like the "Big Brother/Big Sister" program give underprivileged children a chance to learn life skills from someone who has already been there, wherever "there" may be. Maybe it's teaching people how to use their hands or learn how to use carpentry tools, or even how to use a computer. Again, these options would depend on the skills of the people who are interested in doing this particular ministry. Cooking classes are always an option or making do with less. The possibilities for instruction are almost endless but should be based on the needs of your area or parish community.

I know of a church locally who really went out of the way to make this particular issue an important part of what they do. They have a program set up with the local schools to issue a point system. For each day the child is in school, he receives a point. At Christmas time, the points go toward Christmas presents. Donors, all local merchants, donate new items for Christmas. With the accrued points, the

Social Justice

child's family can come in and "shop" for Christmas presents based on the number of points the child earned through the school year. This is brilliant! It keeps the children in school and helps them get Christmas presents when their families are low income and otherwise couldn't afford those things. Yes, this is very involved to coordinate but also very effective outreach.

Another local church collects backpacks and/or school supplies for low income children to enable them to have the tools they need to get back to school at the beginning of the year.

Another opportunity to stay connected with those in school is to send birthday cards and care packages from the parish to students away at college. This would keep them tied to the parish.

Comforting the sorrowful - Within this sphere, you can provide various programs to the grieving. You may want to have a support group, if you have the professional abilities available. You can offer a widows and widowers singles meet club. You may want to have a group of people assist with food preparation for the days immediately following the funeral for a while. You may even want to have a group of people that come to pray with the grieving person or maybe just visit and take them out for groceries, or spend time with them if they need company. No two people's grief is the same. It's about making the connection with them individually and seeing what they need at that particular time. But, more than anything else, it's about being present to someone and sharing in their grief with love and compassion. This would be under an umbrella of bereavement ministry.

Bearing wrongs patiently - The only thing that comes to mind is offering classes on anger management and the power of forgiveness. Teaching about God's patient and inviting mercy might be helpful here as well. Assisting with existing victim support groups or counselling services may be a good way to get involved.

Admonishing the sinner - This may involve some sort of counseling services. Or it could include offering classes for your own improvement where you learn to give constructive criticism versus destructive and hurtful criticisms that may, in effect, stunt any potential spiritual growth. Parent and teenager communication classes come to mind to help in communications and understanding between the groups. You could also include family oriented projects that get people working together and talking to each other. Maybe you can resolve to rake the leaves of an area where you know they are all elderly and have everyone go as a group with each family being responsible for a particular section. You could even do prizes for the most helpful. These activities, while not admonishing the sinner are doorways to constructive communication and positive role modeling. You could also offer programs which explain Church teaching on sin and God's mercy.

Social Justice

Forgiving all injuries - Here, I think I would offer classes and small group discussions on various aspects of our Catholic faith. Forgiveness takes a lot of practice. Having a good spiritual foundation would be beneficial here. In this particular case, I think that this work of mercy would fall under improving the church from within.

Praying for the living and the dead - Praying is easy, or at least it should be. It doesn't cost anything except time. Prayer is also the main foundation upon which this book and the work of Evangelization are based.

> *Blessed are you when they insult you and persecute you and utter every kind of evil against you falsely because of me. Rejoice and be glad for your reward will be great in heaven. Thus they persecuted the prophets who were before you.*

Welcome to the world of Evangelization. Just remember you can't please everyone so be sure you are on track with God. Persecutions and naysayers for your actions will be plentiful. Hopefully so will the fruits of your persistence. Have faith and pray for God's protection and guidance over you.

I hope you have found this section helpful for some ideas to get you started.

12

Final Thoughts

This, my last chapter, is one on final thoughts.

The examples of my mistakes in this book may seem obvious to some of you but I had to learn them from the school of hard knocks and that's why I wanted to share my experiences with you because maybe my lessons will serve to help someone. Even with all the mistakes and mishaps, I can't begin to explain to you the feeling of joy that comes from knowing that God has used you and your presence and your words to touch someone else's heart. It is that peace and that joy that keeps us all going out and trying different ways to connect with others. Some of the things we try work, others not so well or need some tweaking. But through it all, there is an invigorating, deep knowing that God's hand is upon you as you go forward in faith to reach out to others. I could never understand how St. Paul would be beaten, tossed into prison, thrown out of town, stoned etc. and keep trudging. Now I know. Evangelization and spreading the Word becomes so much a part of you that connecting with others becomes a longing deep in your bones that you can't outrun, or get away from or ignore but respond to actively in whatever way you can. Now I get it.

Donna Phipps

Many books on Evangelization have included only the positives or potentials for success. It was my hope in writing this book to provide you with concrete ideas and also the realistic outlook. My hope is that this book is helpful and informative to you without discouraging your initiative and efforts. I have included some checklists for you in the appendices of this book. The first is one in Appendix A is a Best Practices checklist which will let you look at your parish with the eyes of a stranger and let you do a "welcoming" assessment. As with all things in ministry, be honest with yourselves and each other as you go through it. Don't just see the things you take for granted. Look at things with the eyes of a stranger who may be coming for the first time. How would they see you? It may give you some places that need adjustment or correction, some new goals for your efforts. The second checklist I have included in Appendix B is one that can be tailored for event planning. The one I included is not very detailed but is the starting point to which other things can be added or deleted based on your particular needs. The chapter on Event Planning is more detailed for various preliminary aspects, as well as, last minute and planning details that could be addressed. I know that sometimes people find it difficult to know where to begin an event. Talk it through and determine as a group what you want to do and who will do what. I have included a sample Needs Assessment in Appendix C, a sample phone survey in Appendix D and questions to get conversations started in Appendix E. I am

Final Thoughts

also available to you, should you have any questions I didn't cover here specifically. Please email me at info@fishersonthestreet.org. I check this email every day.

Last thought. Don't be discouraged, keep up the God and good work. Don't give up. Remain flexible and not rigid in your thinking so that God can use you. Be prepared to deal with disasters as they occur and don't give in to despair or frustration. Keep a mental back-up plan just in case things don't go as planned. Keep joy in your hearts and may God grant wings to your feet. God bless you all.

Appendix A

Best Practices Checklist

I am including a Best Practices checklist here. This is a good way to look at your parish through the eyes of a stranger to see what they might see, both the good and the things that may need to be adjusted. Some of the questions may not be applicable to your particular parish community.

Best Practices Checklist for Parishes

Hospitality/Welcome

1. Are there any greeters?

    Yes _____ No_____

    (If no move to question 2)

    a. What actions are they performing? (handing out bulletins, handing out song sheets or readings for the week, or something else like prayer cards) _____ _____

    b. How many are there?_____

    c. Are there one or more per door?

    Yes_____ No_____

d. Are they smiling?

   Yes_____ No_____

   e. Are they enthusiastic?

   Yes_____ No_____

   f. Did greeters recognize newcomers

   Yes _____ No_____

   g. Did the greeters suggest that newcomers enter their names and email addresses on something?

   Yes _____ No_____

2. Is there a gathering space for before and after Mass?

   Yes _____ No_____

   (If no move to question 3)

   a. Is the area well lit?

   Yes _____ No_____

   b. Is the area unobstructed and clutter free?

   Yes _____ No _____

   c. Is the hospitality area clean and inviting?

   Yes _____ No_____

   d. Is there enough food and drink and utensils, etc.?

   Yes _____ No_____

3. Is there some form of hospitality after Mass?

    Yes _____ No_____

    (if no move onto next section)

  a. How often is hospitality offered?

    Weekly _____

    Monthly _____

    Quarterly _____

    Seldom _____

    Never _____

    Unknown _____

  b. Who is invited to attend hospitality functions? (for example entire parish, a specific group of those who were baptized during the preceding year, those who retired in the year etc.) _____

_____

_____

_____

Bulletin

4. Are meetings for the week prominently posted?

    Yes _____ No_____

5. Are upcoming events and projects posted and explained in detail?

    Yes _____ No_____

6. Are there listings for many of the major ministries of the parish including, but not limited to, catechesis, school issues, youth and adult activities, Mass times and changes, if any?

        Yes _____ No_____

7. Is there an invitation for others to join the ministries in the bulletin?

        Yes _____ No_____

8. Is there basic contact information in the bulletin?

        Yes _____ No_____

  a. Is there an email address?

        Yes _____ No_____

  b. Is there a parish website?

        Yes _____ No_____

Website

  9. Does the parish have a website?

        Yes ___ No____ Unknown ____

        (If no go to next section)

  a. Is the bulletin included on the website?

        Yes _____ No_____

  b. Is the information on the website up to date?

        Yes _____ No_____

c. Is the website easy to navigate?

　　　Yes _____ No_____

d. Is contact and address information prominent?

　　　Yes _____ No_____

e. Is there a link to the website from the Diocesan home page?

　　　Yes _____ No_____

Music Ministry

10. What is the music style offered during Mass? (i.e. traditional, contemporary, choir, soloist)

_____

11. What type of instrumental accompaniment is there to the music? (folk group, organist, pianist)

_____
_____
_____
_____

12. Are the musicians and singers enthusiastic?

　　　Yes _____ No_____

13. Do the music/singers inspire participation? (shown if a large portion of the congregation sings along, uses bodily movement, clapping, etc.)?

　　　Yes _____ No_____

14. Does choir director make an effort to lead congregation in the singing?

        Yes _____ No_____

15. Does the music foster reverence for the celebration of the Mass?

        Yes _____ No_____

16. Are there sufficient hymnals for everyone?

        Yes _____ No_____

17. Are hymnals easy to locate?

        Yes _____ No_____

Worship Aids

18. Are there missals or cards available with the changes in the Mass?

        Yes _____ No_____

19. Are the words to the songs or song listings and other Mass parts displayed prominently (on overhead display) or announced clearly?

        Yes _____ No_____

Environmental Factors

20. Are entrance ways and church areas well lit?

        Yes _____ No_____

21. Are the walkways and parking lot adequately cleared of ice and snow, free from obstruction and intact?

        Yes _____ No_____

22. Is there an umbrella stand for wet umbrellas?

    Yes _____ No_____

23. Is there a non-slip mat by the entrances during wet or rainy weather?

    Yes _____ No_____

24. Are the microphones used for the lectors and priest at adequate volume and static free?

    Yes _____ No_____

25. Is there a handicap accessibility ramp?

    Yes _____ No_____

26. Is there sufficient room for the handicapped to come in with their chairs and equipment?

    Yes _____ No_____

27. Are the entrances to the church clearly marked?

    Yes _____ No_____

28. Is there adequate signage from the road?

    Yes _____ No_____

    a. Does the sign have the correct name and location of the church?

       Yes _____ No_____

    b. Does the external signage list current Mass times, if space allows?

       Yes _____ No_____

c. Does the external signage have a quote or inspirational thought for passersby?

Yes _____ No_____

29. Is there adequate seating available?

Yes _____ No_____

30. Is there sufficient room in between rows?

Yes _____ No_____

31. Is there adequate parking?

Yes _____ No_____

32. Is the temperature adequately cool or warm (depending on the time of year) for the church and gathering areas?

Yes _____ No_____

Liturgical Aspects

33. Is there a wide age range of participants in the congregation?

Yes _____ No_____

a. Are there a significant number of youth and young adults present?

Yes _____ No_____

b. Does the homilist engage the congregation with thought-provoking questions?

Yes _____ No_____

34. Does the homilist ask for audience participation during his homily (show of hands, or a specific question)?

Yes _____ No_____

35. Does the homilist stay behind the pulpit or come into the congregation? _____
_____
_____

36. Does the homilist use any humor in his homily?

Yes _____ No_____

Administrative

37. What is the process for registering with the parish? _____
_____

   a. Is the registration process easy? (i.e., a tear-off from the bulletin put in the collection basket)

   b. Do all the different ministries receive the necessary information when a new parishioner/family registers?

Yes _____ No_____

(if no proceed to next numbered question)

if Yes, what is the process for communication and dissemination of information? _____
_____

38. Do the staff or priest make some type of overture to welcome new families (either in the bulletin, phone call, email, personal letter or other invitation)

        Yes_____No_____

If Yes, what is done? _____
_____
_____
_____

39. If an email or question is entered in the website, where does it go? _____
_____
_____
_____

    a. Who responds to it? _____

    b. How long before a response is received by the person inquiring? _____
_____
_____

    c. Are phone calls to the office returned in a timely manner?

        Yes _____ No_____

40. Have the mass times and locations, as posted in the bulletin and on the website, been checked and verified?

        Yes _____ No_____

41. How are volunteers treated? _____
_____
_____
_____
_____
_____
_____

Last thoughts

42. Would visitors find a reason to return?

Appendix B
Sample Checklist for Event Planning

Here is my checklist I used when we brought the theologian to speak with us.

Volunteers

Parking (11 people needed)

Ticket taking (6 needed)

Food service (5?)

Setup/Cleanup (5?)

Book/video sellers (4)

Cleaning garbages during event (3)

Keeping toilet paper and paper towels stocked (3)

Get volunteers through bulletin announcement

Meeting for volunteers one week prior to event

Get contact info/cell phones for volunteers for communication ease (like walkie talkies, cell phones, etc.)

Local Catholic High School involvement and or Youth Ministry program

Other volunteer items: _____
_____
_____
_____

Parking

Sign for Bus stop

Maps of off-site location

Itinerary to Bus drivers

Contract for Bus and payment

Clean parking lot

Signs to the offsite parking facilities

posted on street lamps

Other parking items: _____
_____
_____
_____

Advertising

Local Catholic Newspaper event advertisement section

Event Programs

Print tickets and parking maps

Set up ticket recording and disbursement system in database

Local Catholic Radio

All churches within diocese for church bulletins

All surrounding diocese main communication offices for dissemination

Other advertising items: _____

_____
_____
_____

City

City permits if needed

Police and barricades for day of event if needed

EMT for stand by

Other City items:_____

_____
_____
_____

Supplies

Toilet paper

Paper towels

Mud mats for doorways if it rains

Tables/chairs at each of the entrances for volunteers

Keys to storage areas to access supplies for the church and the hall

Other supply items: _____

_____

_____

Presenter

Set date and Contract with office

Purchase plane tickets

Make hotel reservations?

Make arrangements for books

Make arrangements for audio materials

Pick up from the airport and delivery to

Who?/When? _____

_____

Shipping of left over materials

Other presenter items: _____

_____

_____

_____

Food

Contract with caterer

Decide what you will be serving and what time

Work out the dates when he needs final numbers of attendees and payment

Other food items:_____
_____
_____
_____

Additional activities

Small ensemble players for musical interlude while waiting for speaker to arrive

Someone to lead in pre-event rosary and Divine Mercy chaplet _____

Other activity items:_____
_____
_____
_____
_____

Appendix C

Sample Parish Needs Assessment Survey

This is a survey I conducted at one of the parishes I belonged to. Please feel free to tweak it as appropriate for your needs.

> *"And if riches be a desirable possession in life, what is more rich than Wisdom which produces all things?...[N]othing in life is more useful to men than this" (Wisdom 8:5,7).*

The newly formed Adult Education Board of St Mary's is sending out this survey to get your input regarding your religious educational and faith building needs. Based upon your responses, we will create a program to meet the needs expressed. Our goal is to help you learn more about the Catholic faith and to continue to grow closer to God in the process.

Please return the answered survey to the rectory, or in the baskets provided in the back of the church, by _____. All your responses are appreciated and will be helpful as we form the direction of the Adult Education program in this parish.

1. Do you want to know more about the Catholic faith?

    _____Yes _____ No

2. Do you feel a need to get closer to God?

    _____Yes _____ No

If you answered no to both of these questions, you do not need to go any further. Please submit your responses to the rectory. If you answered yes to either question, please continue with the survey.

3. Which areas do you feel you would like to know more about? Please check off the areas you may be most interested in. Please mark a #1 next to your most preferred choice.

    ____Faith similarities and differences between Catholics and Protestants

    ____Church teachings and moral stance

    ____Church history

    ____A study of scripture

    ____Ecumenism and missionary service

    ____Judaic tradition, history and study of the old testament

    ____Meaning and format of the liturgy

    ____In depth look at the sacraments

    ____Lives of the saints

4. What type of learning style best suits you (please mark your top 3 choices)

    ____Formal lectures

    ____Video/audio tapes

    ____Informal assemblies with selected guest speakers

    ____Small discussion groups

    ____Question and answer sessions

    ____Retreats lasting several hours/days

5. Would you want to know more about the following areas? (Please check all that apply)

    ____Centering prayer

    ____Charismatic prayer

    ____Communal prayer

    ____Novenas

    ____Chaplets and other devotions

    ____The rosary

    ____Scriptural meditation

    ____Understanding the way the Holy Spirit works

6. How many times per month would you be willing to attend these programs if offered? (Please check one box only.)

    ____more than once a week

    ____one time per week

    ____two times a month

    ____once a month

7. What time of day would be best for you to attend church-sponsored events?

    ____mornings

    ____afternoon

    ____early evening to end by 9PM

8. If child care were provided for your children, would you be more able to attend this program?

    ____Yes _____ No _____N/A

9. If you have any additional comments, suggestions or other items you would like to share, or if you feel there is an area we have not addressed, please write them here. All your comments are valuable and appreciated.

_____
_____
_____
_____
_____

(Optional) If you would like to be contacted to discuss your faith needs or to share your ideas, please include your name and phone number here.

Name: _____

Phone number: _____

What is the best time to reach you? _____
_____

Thank you for taking the time to answer this survey. God bless you.

Appendix D

Sample Phone Survey

Here is an example of a quick survey that can be made of parishioners over the phone. This procedure can be labor intensive but you will also get a higher percentage of people to respond and you can tabulate the results faster. Another option is instead of calling all the families in the parish, you could also choose to randomly pick let's say 30% and call only those families. The way you do this is entirely up to you based on what you are trying to accomplish. What I have below is a guideline only. At the time we made this, we were looking for reasons why people were not attending Mass and to update the parish address record.

Hello, my name is _____

I'm calling from St. Mary's Parish. We are calling everyone in the parish so that we can update our records.

Administrative Questions

Can you verify that you still live at the same address (read off address)?

Would you like to continue to receive mailings?

Would you like to receive information by email rather than mail?(if yes what is your email address? _____)

How many people are in your household and what are the ages?_____
_____

Optional Questions

(At any point, if they don't want to answer all the questions you can jump down to the final question)

1. Would you like to answer a few questions about St. Mary's Church? (if yes continue with this section, if no jump to final question) (please check one)

____Yes ____No

2. Are you still attending Mass at St. Mary's Parish?

____Yes ____No

(If not, why not?) _____
_____

3. Our parish is offering a program that has been developed to answer some of the concerns you may have about the church. Would you be interested in receiving more information on this?

____Yes ____No

4. Are you able to get to church on a regular basis?

____Yes ____No

____<1 weekend per month

____1-4 Weekends per month

____Don't want to answer

5. Do you have a physical impediment to your attendance (lack of transportation, etc.)

____Yes ____No

If yes, please explain _____

_____

_____

6. Do you feel connected to other members in the parish?

____Yes ____No

7. Are you involved in any ministries?

____Yes ____No

8. What do you like about St. Mary's Parish?

_____

_____

_____

9. What do you dislike about St. Mary's parish?

_____

_____

_____

10. Is there something St. Mary's parish could do for you to improve your life in any area?

____Yes ____No

If yes, please explain. _____
_____
_____
_____

11. Is there something St. Mary's parish could do for you to improve your spiritual life?

        ____Yes ____No

(Ask for some comment to explain either answer)
_____
_____
_____
_____

12. Is there anything else you would like to say or comment on?

        ____Yes ____No

(If yes, would you like someone to contact you regarding your current concerns?)

        ____Yes* ____No

13. Final Question: Is there something you would like us to pray for? _____
_____
_____
_____
_____

* *Please note*, it is EXTREMELY important that you follow up with this person if they say they want to talk to someone. Make the initial call and then follow-up again to make sure their needs were met or questions answered. Leaving someone without an answer will leave a bad feeling and grow distrust or bitterness toward the Church and those in ministry. One or two follow-ups on the other hand will grow a trust relationship. Don't say you are going to do something and not do it. That would be really bad form and just plain rude. It makes the other person feel that their questions or concerns don't matter. Another thing is to make sure you do a timely follow-up. If you allow several weeks to pass, the person will have forgotten their need and just remember your lack of response.

Appendix E

General Questions to Get Conversations Started

Here are some more questions we came up with. These might be good to ask people in small group discussions or if you call a church meeting of all parishioners to get their input for upcoming projects. If you hold a church meeting, be sure you have someone recording, whether by writing down or with an actual recording device, what people's responses are to these (or your own) questions. This also is a quick way to get results but it takes some pre-planning to reserve the church and to announce it far enough ahead so people can attend.

Do you feel your faith needs to be enriched?

What types of programs would be useful to you?

Do you feel like you are a part of your parish?

In what part of your parish community do you feel your talents are most useful?

How does your parish build community?

In your parish, what kind of music would make you want to sing?

Are you part of a ministry?

How do you share your faith at work?

How do you share your faith at home?

How do you share your faith in your daily routines?

How do you share your faith socially?

Epilogue
Last Laugh

A few years ago, the diocese asked the Catholic school children to create life-sized plywood cutouts of saints. Each school was given one saint as their assignment. The diocese then used these cut out saints during their annual adult education week in the spring. When the event was over, the saints were up for grabs for anyone who wanted them. I received the email and asked for St. Paul. Since the Street Evangelization group was St. Paul Street Evangelization, the actual St. Paul was an evangelizer to the nations and on missionary journeys, it made sense to have him as part of our entourage. I didn't know why we needed him, just that we did. I emailed the sender of the email and said I wanted Paul. He responded that he was already claimed. WHAT?!?!?!?! How was that possible?!?!?!?!?!?!? I had emailed within minutes of the message coming in. The diocesan contact slipped up and told me who had claimed them. My normally gentle and graceful nature gave way to the on-the-trail cyber stalker where I was unswerving in my resolve until I tracked these figures down. I emailed the people who had laid claim to Paul and asked if we could have him. They could keep the rest. Joy of joys! They said yes!!!

Carol and I did a raid at the diocesan pastoral center to extricate our prize as if we had just won some battle and major victory to attain him. She laid a hold of this cut out figure that towered over her head and walked him to the elevator. All you could see were little feet moving as fast as they could under Paul, blinded by his stature. It really looked like some sort of animation as he moved through the hallway. We got him down to the car and I couldn't get the trunk open! Something had jammed the release. How was I going to get this thing home? I also realized that I had brought the really small car. I certainly didn't want to leave my prize at the pastoral center because I didn't know if it would still be there upon my return with another vehicle. Sigh. Now what? I put all the seats down, pulled the driver's seat and passenger seats forward as far as they would go and started to maneuver Paul into the car. I pushed and pulled, first on one side then the other. I thought for sure I was going to snap his head off but I finally got him into the car. Carol was all hunched forward and just about sitting on the dashboard but we were all in! We are nothing if not determined.

The Street Evangelization team has permission to be at the airport so that we can interact with people there. We bring Paul with us. It really is eye-catching and a conversation starter. Some people say it's St. Francis, others say Santa Claus but either way, he is now on his fourth missionary journey with us. The airport staff are getting used to seeing us with him. They even make jokes that only human passengers are allowed on the shuttle and everyone else who can't be strapped in (meaning Paul) is to remain behind. Then there was the time when the wind picked up and carried Paul through the parking lot several feet before he landed with a loud crash. I thought he broke at that time too but he's survived so far. And the adventure continues...

Our street evangelization setup at the airport with Paul.